The Man with Nine Lives

The Man with Nine Lives

A Search for Evidence of Reincarnation

by
Doris Patterson

A.R.E. Press • Virginia Beach • Virginia

1st Printing, June 1994

Printed in the U.S.A.

A.R.E. Press
Sixty-Eighth & Atlantic Avenue
P.O. Box 656
Virginia Beach, VA 23451-0656

Grateful acknowledgment is made to the following publishers for permission to reprint from their publications:
Many Lives, Many Masters, copyright 1988 by Brian L. Weiss. Simon & Schuster. Used by permission.
Through Time into Healing, copyright 1992 by Brian L. Weiss. Simon & Schuster. Used by permission.
Other Lives, Other Selves, copyright 1987 by Roger Woolger. Doubleday. Used by permission.

Library of Congress Cataloging-in-Publication Data
Patterson, Doris, 1917-
The man with nine lives : a search for evidence of reincarnation / by Doris Patterson.
p. cm.
Includes bibliographical references.
ISBN 0-87604-325-2
1. Turner, Albert, 1907-1968. 2. Reincarnation—United States—Case studies. I. Title.
BL520.T47P38 1994
133.9'01'3-dc20 94-15823

Cover design by Lightbourne Images

For Gladys

The angel of Al's life

Contents

Acknowledgments

As a tree owes its growth to the soil, air, water, and sun, this book owes its existence to many friends to whom I must express heartfelt appreciation:

Bill and Lois Ann Newlin, for the discovery of the reels of wire recordings, for sharing numerous books, for turning the reels of wire into cassette recordings;

Hadassah Roberts, first for saving her careful cache of recordings, and second for her good-humored sharing of memories of Dr. George;

Marianne Wolf, for sharing *her* memories of Dr. George and the Theosophists;

Michael Schwager, for untangling some computer knots;

S. C. Antholz, for her sources of information on England and its rulers in the 1500s and 1600s;

Peter Hewitt, editor, the National Publishing Company, for the detailed information on the translating of the King James Version of the Bible;

Betsy Hoffman, for sharing her books and encouragement;

Robert Swartz, president of the Lower Merion Historical Society, for Civil War Army Units and other information;

All my children for their help and encouragement;

The staff of Ludington Library, Bryn Mawr, particularly the Research Librarian, for assistance in so many items from ancient coins to Siberian mammals;

And to the many friends whose patience and encouragement made a difference.

Introduction

The story you are about to read is true. Only the times have changed. Today people don't think it's so strange to speak about past lives.

"Past lives" is a simpler, clearer term for most of us than the five-syllable "reincarnation," from the Latin meaning "back in the body again." It is based on the belief that a soul may inhabit one body after another. This belief, known around the world for thousands of years, has not only been featured recently in books, films, and television, but put to practical use as well.

For example, Brian L. Weiss, M.D., Florida psychiatrist, with his best-selling *Many Lives, Many Masters* and *Through Time into Healing,* since 1988 has been acclaimed by the media and by many in the medical profession as well, for his insights on healing clients through the use of past-life regressions.

The past-life concept for healing was also well shown by psychologist Roger J. Woolger, whose *Other Lives, Other Selves* was written in 1987 from a Jungian view of past-life regression therapy and the body-mind relationship. It is the need for healing, rather than simple curiosity, that is turning more people today to searching such long-ago experiences.

It was back in 1950 that Dr. Gina Cerminara wrote *Many Mansions,* an account of past lives based not on the hypnotic regressions of individuals but on "readings" or clairvoyant trance sessions given by Edgar Cayce, the "sleeping prophet."

Cayce, born the son of a Kentucky farmer in 1877, had an ability to diagnose illnesses and prescribe remedies while in an unconscious state. This ability appeared when, as a young insurance salesman, he had lost his voice. A traveling hypnotist put him in a trance and asked about the problem. The hypnotized Cayce, with an eighth-grade education, spoke as a medical doctor giving the source and the solution to his problem. Later he learned to put himself in a trance and answer questions with what were called "readings," for people who asked for his help. He was even headlined by the *New York Times* in 1910 for the accuracy of his readings. A decade later, a businessman interested in the reach of the unconscious and in metaphysics asked for information on life guidance. Cayce was shocked to learn afterward that in trance he had indicated that reincarnation was a strong influence and had described former lives. When he was given a person's birth date and the request to tell the "former appearances on the earth plane," from his trance would come "life readings" which told of a man's or woman's past lives which were affecting the present. These were given in some detail and became a help in understanding relationships and goals.

Although Edgar Cayce died in 1945, some of the men and women he had "read" for were still alive when *Many Man-*

sions was published in 1950. But the past lifetimes described by Edgar Cayce in Dr. Cerminara's book did not make the person-in-the-street feel directly connected to the possibility of his or her own past and future existence. Even if they had wanted to, people could not consult Edgar Cayce because the seer was no longer alive.

Perhaps this was why *Many Mansions*—though widely read—did not create a firestorm of criticism and objections from some religious denominations who feel their foundations threatened if anyone hints that people who die don't go at once to heaven or hell, but may be "born again" on earth.

In 1956, however, when Morey Bernstein's *The Search for Bridey Murphy* became the newspapers' and the talk shows' favorite topic, there was an earthquake of indignation from many orthodox religionists, who went to great lengths—including more than misstatements—to prove it couldn't have happened. Despite the detailed investigations and confirmations by *Denver Post* writer/investigator William Barker, they were unmoved. No hypnotized Colorado housewife could possibly recall a real lifetime as an Irish lass born in 1798.

In 1965, when Dr. Leslie Weatherhead, head of the City Temple in London, was ready to publish *The Christian Agnostic*, which contains a delightful chapter titled "Reincarnation and Renewed Chances," he felt it necessary to resign his church position.

In 1966, when noted psychiatrist Ian Stevenson, M.D., of the University of Virginia, published his thoroughly documented research in *Twenty Cases Suggestive of Reincarnation*, there still seemed to be the general feeling that the concept was somehow heretical and writers should apologize for mentioning it.

Certainly there were ancient authors, including Plato and Pythagoras, who wrote of reincarnation and a few biblical scholars who quoted chapter and verse[1] to show it was an approved concept to early Christians and some nineteenth- and twentieth-century writers, scholars, and philosophers such as Hume, Kant, Schopenhauer, and Jung who accepted it. But authors who were considered intellectual or abstruse had little impact on the popular mind. There was an occasional exception when someone with scientific credentials would "debunk" some claim of the paranormal with circus-like fanfare. That, the conservative media might accept, while deploring the gullibility of the public.

Consequently, in 1952 when Henry George, III, D.O., worked as a hypnotist with past-life regression, he did not advertise it to the general public, only to those already involved in the study of the mystical or paranormal. He, himself, was a member of the Theosophical Society, which focused on such topics, and of the Association for Research and Enlightenment (A.R.E.), based in Virginia Beach, whose purpose was to foster the work and study begun by Edgar Cayce. Dr. George had gone to the A.R.E. in the early 1940s after a man brought him a diagnosis from the seer, to learn how Edgar Cayce had made it; he came as a challenger, but left as a friend. Now Dr. George was hoping his own research would uncover verifiable proof of past lives. What he wanted was data that would fit historical fact. Helping a personality to heal was not a stated part of his plan.

Still we do have the records, the transcripts of the unadvertised, private sessions with Albert Turner in 1952. Also we have some recordings of the subject under hypnosis speaking, even chanting or singing, in different types of voices. And it is clear that he was a different, far happier man afterward.

So three questions come to mind: How did we get the records? What do they tell us? What does it mean?

How did we get them? That is a story in itself.

What they told us, you will find in the coming chapters.

What does it mean? You will see what it meant to Albert

Turner, and you will judge what it might mean for you.

The first work with this material went into a biography of Albert Turner for family and friends who knew him. But the subject of his past lives was touched only briefly. Since then, more study and research has provided additional facts on background as well as more significance to the patterns he experienced in those lives which made such a change afterward.

First, it may be helpful to know some of what went into the background work for this book.

PREPARATION FOR THE SEARCH

To learn more, to view Al's story in a clearer context, I researched several areas: hypnosis, past-life regression—including a personal experience with it—multiple personalities, and a deeper look at time periods and eras of Al's nine lives.

I studied about hypnosis and went through a regression myself; I read even more widely about past-life regression, spoke with some friends who had remembered past lives. Then there were those who specialized in the field, such as Dr. Helen Wambach with her regressions of many groups of subjects, stopping at certain time periods. There was Dr. Roger Woolger, a clinical psychologist who specialized in past-life regression, who presented a view of the multidimensional psyche from several sides. He made it clear, however, that memories of past lives—like memories from past decades—may also contain "some degree of confabulation."[2] But the literal existence of the past life, whether it occurred with the details exactly as described, was not the moving force for change. It was the inner work, the person's emotional reactions within the past-life setting, that seemed to bring adjustment, healing changes, not just psychological but often physical as well.

The books of Dr. Brian L. Weiss, *Many Lives, Many Masters* and *Through Time into Healing*, opened up other aspects of past lives also. Dr. Weiss had found "masters" within several of his subjects, higher beings who could see everything that was going on and, if asked, offer a needed perspective on a life and relationships.

Most of the regressed subjects lost not only their phobias or other symptoms, but their fear of death as well.

Another facet not considered in 1952 when the doctor had worked with Al was multiple personalities—increasingly being studied now as multiplicities of "normal" people. It is a new idea to many, although brought out nearly a century ago by William James, American psychologist-philosopher. It was the central topic of Dr. James Fadiman, speaking on "Personal Multiplicities" at the First International Congress on Healing Beyond Sickness and Death.[3] Dr. Fadiman noted that most normal people have other selves, which some call "subpersonalities."

Most people have heard of the pathological multiples, the "Three Faces of Eve," for example, but those did not share their memories, so what one experienced was unknown to the others. It now seems that other selves are frequently active even in the most normal of people. According to Dr. Fadiman, they can be symptoms of "superior mental health." For example, a person could call on his *social* self at a party, his *accounting* self when reconciling a checkbook, other selves with other skills when appropriate. How could one tell if he or she had other selves? One example: When driving somewhere, do you sometimes realize with surprise that you are at your destination—with no recollection of how you got there? There was no robot holding that steering wheel or avoiding oncoming cars. One self was doing the driving, while another was solving a problem or planning a dinner.

In addition to finding multiple or subpersonalities and

"masters" within individuals, some researchers, such as Jack Hilgard at Stanford Hypnosis Laboratory, also found an "observer," an entity who could see and hear what was going on without being confined to the hypnotized personality, but could be contacted separately. This, too, was mentioned by William James. These additional discoveries helped to explain what had first seemed some really strange replies in these sessions.

Within Al Turner's responses could be found both the main identity and a couple of others—sometimes a young and simple lad who liked "the pretty boat, oh, isn't it pretty" and other childish expressions; sometimes a visionary. Often an observer emerged who could see not just as the Civil War soldier or the Italian friar or other person, but could see over the personality walls, could see through time to other periods, including the present. And it also seemed that a master spoke.

To understand more of the experience, I also went through a hypnotic past-life regression and became aware at firsthand of some of the processes. Aspects of self were revealed which I had to acknowledge, but their discovery brought about a new awareness as well as a beneficial change in the present life.

A group of us signed up to be hypnotized together by Dr. Bruce Goldberg at an A.R.E. symposium. We were given the additional instruction that if something traumatic happened to us, we would be outside our body, not upset, but looking on. This can be important for group work, in case one person's entering an active crisis might disturb another. Then we were told to seek out a past life that would have some significance in the present. I saw myself as a man, wearing a brown tunic, brown stockings, working in a print shop in a medieval town, operating a press something like Gutenberg's. I was pleased that I had printed and posted several small placards criticizing a religious leader for oppressing the villagers. While standing in the doorway, I saw the man I was writing about at a distance—then his face with a nasty grin seemed right in front of me. Suddenly I felt a blow on the back. Because of the earlier suggestion, I found myself standing outside my body, looking down at the poor wretch sprawled on the cobblestones, a dagger stuck below his shoulder blade. I understood that the man I had criticized with the posters had arranged my killing.

Applying that to the present, I've been careful since then choosing words when making a criticism of someone or something, staying away from the personal but marshalling the facts. Physically, I noted that the spot where the dagger entered was a place that had been numb, for some unknown reason, all my life. I also understood the phenomenon Al expressed in one of his experiences, where he could observe at a distance and "suddenly I'm right up." For I had just such a "zoom-lens" effect seeing the leader far off, then right in front of me.

Additional research has shone more light on some of the dimmer time periods of Al's sessions, as well as some of the statements that were first assumed to be misconceptions, inaccuracies, or just "off the wall." On several occasions, a bit of digging turned up a little-known quirk of history which made the "impossible" seem probable.

There were occasional errors; for example, giving the wrong altitude for Mt. Carmel or the wrong name for an author (he recalled Valzac when it must have been Balzac), and other times when his numbers and spelling seemed off the mark.

But this is not written as a statistical reference—not even as "proof" of past lives.

This is the story of a man changed by *feeling* those past lives, by *experiencing* the emotions of the events, and by love.

1
Searching for Connections

The stockbroker turned in his swivel chair and picked up the telephone. "I'll be glad to get that for you, Tom. Forty shares, at ten and a half. Yes, that's a fine asset for your portfolio. I'll put it through today—oh, sorry, it's just past three. It will go in first thing Monday."

He hung up the receiver with a smile. Another sale. Not much, but his third one today. Earlier, he'd had to break the news to Mrs. Grey that the stock she wanted to sell was not now worth what she had paid for it. Not a big loss, but it was unfortunate for her. Many people were still nervous about investments even though the big crash was some twenty years in the past, but when you studied the companies and the trends, it wasn't nearly as risky as it had been.

The ticker-tape machines had quieted, and the others in the office were shuffling papers, calling a stenographer, making notes, winding up the activities of the Philadelphia brokerage firm. He wished there were a way to have more control over the stocks and that he could order so many shares and be certain the value would increase with time, that the companies would be even better than they looked in the prospectus, and the clients would be happy with their profit—and he with his commission. It would be nice if there were no risk to investments—but unless you were a king with a full treasury, there would always be some risk.

It was a tough business—but no tougher than some of those he had been in. At least it beat selling vegetables from a truck, as he had done in the middle twenties.

At home he had dinner and began studying for the Servicemen's Bible Class he would teach on Sunday morning. There were plenty of other things to do . . .

But the Bible Class was important. He wasn't sure just why it was so important to him, but he knew he needed to teach it, to talk to the young men of St. Luke's Methodist Church. Especially the men now in the service, going to Korea or elsewhere, so soon to face the question of killing or being killed. God, what a quandary, he thought half prayerfully. He had already had a couple of heart attacks; the doctor had thought he'd be dead within a year of his second one. But he was still here. And he was now physically unfit for military service, but he wanted to do what he could to help the men who were in it.

"Cedar trees? The best cedars? From Tyre, yes, Your Majesty." The commerce secretary checked his scrolls. Solomon had the idea that they should have cedars for the temple he planned. So now there was this shipment to arrange. He didn't have to worry about the cost, but Solomon would know if he paid too much. "Of course, you want the very best, Sire. We can have them cut, loaded, and transported along the coast." Provided no one backed out of his agreement, it ought to go smoothly.

When the king was in a good mood, Onon enjoyed talking with him. "You want this temple to last a long while, right, Sire?" Then he chuckled, "You say somebody is going to come along who will be a deliverer? Deliver what? More trees? With you as our king, we don't need a deliverer." After he got this order finished, Onon would have to send messengers to the harbor. Onon didn't feel like going home to his wife. She always had something to complain about. So he kept working and chuckling. Deliverer, indeed.

"What a cuckoo idea!" said the voice of the hypnotized man.

The physician-hypnotist shut off the wire recorder. Slowly he brought Albert Turner out of his trance. Al sat up, looked around, caught the eye of Gladys Davis, and the two of them exchanged smiles that lit up the room in the former Cayce home that now served as the headquarters of the Association for Research and Enlightenment.

On this morning in June of 1952, the old house sat like a Victorian lady, at the side of Arctic Crescent, its back turned to the little lake where Edgar Cayce had spent time fishing in between the readings he had given before his death in 1945. Just a couple of blocks from the oceanfront at Virginia Beach, it served for now as a center for consultations and study of the records of the seer's work.

Dr. Henry George explained to Hugh Lynn Cayce, the oldest son of Edgar Cayce, that this was the fourth in a series of eight sessions of hypnotic regression to which Al had agreed. Al thought he might have lived before, and Dr. George was amassing a great deal of research material on the subject of past lives with volunteers like Al.

"I believe you met my father," Hugh Lynn said.

"Yes," Dr. George replied with a short laugh. "A man came to see me for treatment, with a diagnosis from your father. I found it hard to believe anyone could do something like that. So I checked the man out before I even looked at the diagnosis—but it was right. So, I came to Virginia Beach to see him and find out what sort of trickery was behind it. I didn't find any trickery." He laughed again. "We spoke several times after that."

Then Dr. George turned to Gladys. "I hope you're not so worried now, Miss Davis. Working with Mr. Cayce as you did, I'm sure you don't really believe that being in a trance might cause trouble."

Gladys's laugh was musical. "It was interesting," she said noncommittally as Al rose from the couch and stepped beside her. Of course, Mr. Cayce had put *himself* in a trance and had offered information that had brought many hundreds of people back to health—and other "readings" had told of past lives for hundreds more. But putting someone like Al in a trance . . . She had wanted to be present at one of these sessions that he had agreed to take part in, so she could see for herself what was happening. During her twenty-two years of writing down what Mr. Cayce said in trance, she knew he was unique, but she worried about side effects from frequent hypnosis of others—particularly the man she soon would marry. With a little help, they had made arrangements, and Dr. George had been willing to have the fourth session here at the Beach. Now, at least she had seen what usually went on.

We need to look between the past and the present to see the start of it all, to find the reasons for Albert Turner's gazing into the distant mirror of past lives, to learn why and how it began. Of course, it is impossible to sketch a complex life in a few paragraphs, but we can at least glimpse some of the strain and the spiritual search, some of the hurting and the healing potential.

Albert E. Turner, Jr., was my uncle, my father's youngest

brother. The early part of his career had been checkered, to put it mildly. Born in 1907, the youngest of five children, Al was nearly killed by a car at age seven. He lay in a coma for three days, according to the newspaper account. His mother and father weren't sure what he was trying to tell them when he came out of the coma. Today they might say he had a "near-death experience."

His father, Albert E. Turner, Sr., was not only a civic leader honored by the city of Philadelphia, one of the founders of its Committee of Seventy, a leader in the Methodist Episcopal church, and co-founder of an investment firm, he was idolized by his family—especially his youngest son. His father's sudden death from a heart attack in 1920 was a thunderous blow. Al, then thirteen, clung to his closest brother, Paul, for support. When Paul was killed in an accident two years later, Al felt ready to explode with anguish.

The only one of five children still home with mother, who was herself saturated with grief, Al managed to stick it out until he graduated from high school in June of 1924. Then he struck out on his own to work off the frustrating sadness by hitchhiking across the country. He had turned down his mother's offer of $400 in pennies she had saved for his college education; at that time it would have paid for at least a year of it.

It was three months later when Al returned home, not to a welcome but to the scorn of his older brother who accused him of shirking his responsibilities. For a time Al tried various jobs, earning a little money playing piano in bars, selling Realsilk hosiery, even vending vegetables from a truck. Then to his family's surprise, he enlisted in the marines in late 1925. I recall his stopping by our house, handsome in his crisp new uniform. We heard of visits to Tripoli and Cuba, but nothing about the reason for his discharge two years later. Was it something about a good-looking marine not keeping away from native girls?

His mother encouraged his marriage to the daughter of a real estate executive who had a good job as a secretary. They set up their apartment. Intelligent and articulate, Al soon joined the sales force of a Philadelphia investment firm. Then came that terrible day in October 1929 and the crash. Savings disappeared. Somehow, they survived through the next few years.

In 1936, there was a baby girl—who lived just three days. His wife plunged into a deep depression; Al was hospitalized for stomach problems. Difficulties mounted. Al looked for answers in various religions and studied several. He had another heart attack in 1937, and this time the doctor gave him a year to live. Before long, it was obvious the marriage was rocky.

Trying to come to terms with the tragedy of their child's death, his wife's subsequent illness, and his own physical frailty, Al began to connect more with the Methodist church (his father had been an outstanding Methodist layman). He had two more heart attacks but somehow kept going. He joined another Philadelphia investment firm. During World War II he also worked with the Red Cross, giving training in handling emergencies and in lifesaving for swimmers. As that war ended and before long was followed by the Korean conflict, Al remained with the Red Cross and continued Sunday mornings teaching the servicemen's Bible Class.

When they came to the Book of Revelation, a friend gave him a copy of *There Is a River*, by Thomas Sugrue, a biography of Edgar Cayce that included some readings about the Bible. Al devoured the book. This was something he had always wanted to believe in, and here was a book saying it was true. Despite his wife's protests, he joined the A.R.E., visited its headquarters in Virginia Beach, and asked for material on the Bible, especially the Book of Revelation. He used it with his Sunday classes. He was not in great physical shape—in fact, he felt weak and tired—but spent as much time as possible on meditation and prayer, hoping for his own revelation. His wife started action for a divorce.

What did the future hold? *Was* there a future? What could develop from his life with so much going wrong? He needed an answer. As an A.R.E. member, he received an announcement that there would be a lecture about past lives and reincarnation at Virginia Beach in January 1952. He went to the lecture. His wife got her divorce.

Our family lost track of him for four years. It was in 1956 that he came to visit because I had written him that my father, his brother Brinkley, was dying of cancer. He came to the house and spoke with my mother and me, as my father lay silent upstairs. Al seemed a different person. With smiling brown eyes beneath the thinning brown hair, he was gentle, confident. He held our hands. "Brinkley will be all right," he said. I thought he had lost his mind. I *knew* it, when my father died two weeks later.

But Al lent me his copy of *There Is a River* before returning to his home in Virginia Beach. And he invited all our family, including our children, to visit him and Gladys during my husband's vacation.

He was, indeed, far different from the old Al Turner.

I did not learn the whole story until after his death. But during our (Bill, me, four youngsters, and a pussycat) vacation visits with them each year at "the Beach," I did learn, much to my surprise, how almost everyone we met knew him as "Smilin' Al" and how some—especially a waitress whose brother he helped—called him "a saint" and how others felt like "Zip" Johnson of the Norfolk Post Office, who wrote that he was "the most remarkable man I have met during my lifetime." What had made this tremendous change?

Meanwhile, I also joined the A.R.E., whose library held many books not available at home; I did some research there and attended conferences when I could. I had heard mentions—no details—of a special experience, that Al had been hypnotized by a doctor and remembered a past life. But no one I knew seemed interested in getting more details about the past. There were just these occasional hints. I wondered, was it too secret to discuss? Or was it only the *present* that counted?

Later, I learned of that January 1952 lecture he attended at the A.R.E. headquarters, a lecture on past lives by Dr. Henry George. After the talk, Dr. George asked if there were any people in the audience who would be willing to help his research by volunteering for past-life regressions.

Al was curious. He volunteered.

He was also avid for more than the members' standard information from the Cayce readings to use with his Bible studies, as well as for some medical information from the trance readings, which numbered over 14,300. Al felt sure he could get the extra material if he went to the headquarters and asked confidently for it. Determined to have it before he left, he made his way to the office of the Association secretary, Gladys Davis. (During Mr. Cayce's lifetime, she had sat nearby taking notes when he gave most of his trance readings and was considered closer to Mr. Cayce than anyone but his family.) When Al saw her, he stopped, almost speechless. Instead of asking for the readings material, he asked her to lunch.

It was, Gladys said later, as if they had known each other before. And within a couple of months they were planning to marry.

But he had agreed to be a volunteer for Dr. George, who wanted eight sessions of hypnosis, biweekly, beginning in May, so they planned to put the wedding off until midsummer.

Those sessions began in May 1952 and ended in August. They were an almost hidden, not-discussed-in-public side of Al. Of course, Gladys, his friends, and some of the A.R.E. leaders, such as Edgar Cayce's son Hugh Lynn Cayce, knew about it—because one of the sessions was held at the A.R.E. headquarters. But the picture of what was happening to him, while he was experiencing these past lives, was hidden—only the *results* were seen by the men and women with whom Al lived and worked, and only a very few of these were the same people who had known him *before* his coming to Virginia Beach.

What happened to Al as a result of these eight sessions, these ventures into nine previous lifetimes? Did he suddenly become healthier and stronger, canceling the effects of his four previous heart attacks? Paradoxically, he became even more active than before but—he had another heart attack! And after a few years, a stroke. But he stayed involved. He kept going, and in a joyful mood. In 1961, Al suffered another stroke, so serious the doctors said he would be permanently disabled. In the beginning they found no movement in his limbs, they weren't even sure he would be able to speak again. Despite the predictions, Gladys was not dismayed—and with her beside him, Al wasn't either. Within three months, Al was not only able to speak, but to get around, although slowly, with a cane.

Al insisted on leading the classes he enjoyed, helping anyone he could whenever he could. Who would expect this from a man who, sixteen years before, was tired, troubled, frail, and depressed . . . a man from a family known for weak hearts? No statistician would expect it, certainly!

Albert Turner, through those last years, was a moving, speaking affirmation of joy.

The subject of past-life regression seemed remote.

On June 27, 1968, he died.

Gladys, to whom Al gave most of the credit for his happiness, had been collecting material about him and gave it to me: his activities, his sayings she loved, copies of *The*

Searchlight (Bulletins for the A.R.E.) for which he had written articles, but still nothing about any regression sessions. The records, she guessed, might be with the doctor—if we could find him. But other things were more important.

Then it turned up: the program from the January 1952 lecture, listing Henry George, III, of Wilmington, Delaware. Some time soon, I said, I would try to find him. But there was no address or phone number, no reason for haste.

One day on an impulse I picked up the telephone, asked long-distance information if there was a number for Dr. Henry George. I dialed. A man's voice answered.

"Doctor George?" I asked.

"This is his son. Doctor George died last month. I've just come to his office to go over his papers." And to see what he could throw out, I understood.

I was sorry, very sorry to hear about Dr. George's death within a couple of weeks of Al's. But, I asked his son, if he happened to find any materials mentioning Albert Turner in hypnotic sessions, would he let me know? A long shot. But he said he would.

In the middle of the following week, a heavy manila envelope came in the mail. Inside was a notebook, containing 112 typewritten pages of the hypnotic sessions, eight in all, with dates, places, and names of witnesses for each session with Dr. Henry George. I nearly fainted.

An hour earlier, a day earlier or later, I would have missed this entirely.

I went through the pages carefully. There were a few places where the words seemed confusing or out of place, a few misspellings, but the rest of it was like dynamite for my interest. If only I could be sure what was meant in those doubtful lines. I kept gathering material for a memoir to Al: his mother's diaries, old letters, photographs. Our family—brothers, sisters, cousins—would be interested because he was the uncle about whom we knew the least.

It was some years later (my husband had died in the meantime) that my friends Bill and Lois Ann Newlin were with several others helping an old friend, Mrs. Erwin (Hadassah) Roberts of Arden, Delaware, to clear out her attic. Since she had been a member of the Theosophical Society, she had a number of records in her attic that were of more than average interest. Among the findings were some old reels of wire recordings (wire recorders were used before tape recorders came on the scene). But the searchers could not play them. It just so happened that Bill Newlin, who made a specialty of collecting "antique electronics," had a broken one which he had hoped to fix. Soon he came across a missing part, met the challenge, and produced one that worked!

My phone rang. It was Bill Newlin.

"We want you to come over and hear what we found on one of those old reels."

I listened as the voice came out. My skin tingled all over. It was Uncle Al! These were actually recordings of three of the regression sessions with Dr. George!

They transferred the recordings to cassette tapes, so that I could take them home and play them at my leisure.

It was fascinating to listen to Al's voice recalling happenings in 1865, in 952, and even around 33 A.D. When I matched the recordings with parts of the transcript, I could see some places where the typist, who knew no foreign languages, had missed or misspelled the terms. And the different emotions showed in the voice, from childlike wonderment and innocent laughter to adult grief and sonorous chanting.

After reading through the transcripts and listening to the tapes, I was excited but cautious. Albert had only a high school education, to the best of my knowledge knew no foreign languages, and had only those two experiences with travel—the hitchhiking trek across country in 1924 and his brief stint in the marines in 1926. Not much to draw on for a panorama of history on three continents during two millennia, if he *wanted* to make it up.

The hypnotized subject in his different lifetimes described some items, some events, which did not seem to fit. When he spoke as an eight-year-old in 1853, he gave the wrong name for the president of the U.S. Speaking as a scared French boy of five, in 1715, when the hypnotist asked if he knew about the French Revolution, he answered, "I don't remember." (The physician might have been trying to test him, since the French Revolution was some seventy years later.) In another life he said he was a son of James I of England—but his name wasn't Charles. As a captain in the Roman army in the third century A.D., he stated that he was the illegitimate son of the pope! Could anyone believe that?

Maybe this was the reason the transcripts lay in Dr. George's drawer for sixteen years.

Dr. George could not see the future, did not know what additional research would uncover, nor did he know what psychiatrist and author Brian L. Weiss concluded, some forty years later, concerning regressions: "In my practice I have found that the fluid, living, seemingly multicolored mixture of actual experience, metaphor, and distortion that occurs in past-life regression is very similar to the mixture that is found in dreams . . .

"The difference is, again in my experience, that in dreams perhaps seventy percent of the dream content consists of symbol and metaphor, fifteen percent consists of actual memory, and the last fifteen percent of distortion or disguise. I have found that in past-life recall, though, the proportions are usually rather different. Perhaps *eighty percent of the past-life experience will consist of actual memory* [italics added], another ten percent of symbol and metaphor, and the last ten percent distortion or disguise."[1]

Knowing that, Dr. George would have been more excited.

Whether the source was from Al, the searcher, from different time frames, or from an "observer," or from a "master"—or all of them—we can decide not just from what Al said, but from what happened to him.

That was a spiritual adventure.

2
What's in a Man?

To get the right answers you have to ask the right questions.

That was just what the Wilmington, Delaware, physician had planned to do, the first time he worked with the forty-four-year-old stockbroker on the evening of May 22, 1952. In his own office, where he had his reference material, he would place this volunteer in a trance and find out what recall there might be of experiences in previous lives. There were to be at least seven more sessions. Al had leaned back on the couch in the doctor's office, relaxed, and closed his eyes. Dr. George began speaking gently, soothingly, and soon they knew Al was asleep.

The five witnesses sat silent in the background. Members of the Theosophical Society, they had been present at several of Dr. George's previous hypnotic sessions. Some had also taken part in them. They knew the process, but they were never sure just what was going to come out next.

Henry George, III, D.O., was a careful man with a reputation for responsibility. For research into this area, he wanted the most trustworthy witnesses, and he wanted the sessions recorded as well. Dealing with such "unproven" phenomena as past lives, he should have the most reliable records possible.

Besides being a physician, he had studied hypnosis and past-life regression for some years. Recently he had even given pointers to young Morey Bernstein, a writer and hypnotist who was considering writing a book and had visited the doctor a few times. Dr. George had often spoken about his investigations and their results to groups who were open to this area of thinking.

The fact that Dr. George was a member of the Theosophical Society was helpful. Though the name was originally synonymous with mysticism, in the late 1870s it was adopted by an American group interested in combining mystic doctrines of the East and West, including Hindu, Pythagorean, cabalistic, Egyptian, even Buddhist. Mme. Helene Blavatsky, a spirited Russian woman fascinated with these doctrines and ancient legends, had written a book, *Isis Unveiled,* delving deeply into such mystic studies. The Theosophical Society, now over a half century later, had different groups, which continued studying aspects of humankind as spirit. People of different occupations and backgrounds, they felt a need to search and share information. They rarely spoke to outsiders about their group, which was natural considering the times.

We talk of being "politically correct" today in order to get along. Some have forgotten—if they ever knew—that it was quite uncomfortable in the 1950s for people who dared to think or speak anything not considered "correct." U.S. senator Joe McCarthy cast a long shadow over many activities, mainly any which were pro-peace and anti-war, but there were suspicions of *anything* which was not part of standard mainstream beliefs, mother and apple pie. He and J. Edgar Hoover worked at keeping America "sanitary." So these theosophists were cautious about what they said to the uninitiated. But they continued to be active in studying mystical experiences, Eastern philosophies and Western thought, and reincarnation—the belief that a soul after death may be born again some time later in another body. These men and women in the Philadelphia-Wilmington area were quite interested in Dr. George's work of looking for proof of past lives and were more than willing to have meetings—unadvertised—at his office or one of their homes. Then *after* the meeting they would be witnesses to his hypnotic regressions.

Other groups with similar "undercover" interests were forming. Dr. George had found another subject, a Delaware housewife, Zoe Nickerson, who was able under hypnosis to give information on a whole spectrum of material, from files locked in the physician's office to experiences in other worlds. Working with him, she soon found she was able to put herself in a trance and give helpful information to others. From her work, in four more years, Parastudy, Inc., was to be founded: a group interested in psychic studies. Originally in Brookside, Delaware, it is today a source of speakers and classes in psychic phenomena, in Chester Heights, Pa., a little north of Wilmington, although Zoe is no longer connected with it.

The sleeping subject this evening was a man none of them had known until he approached Dr. George after that January lecture at the Association for Research and Enlightenment. The man had come up and volunteered to take part in the experimental hypnotic regressions, because he felt that he had lived before. Albert Turner admitted he had done a lot of reading about religions, Eastern as well as

Western, highlights from Buddhism, Zoroastrianism, the Masonic, Hermetic, cabalistic, and Rosicrucian studies also covered in Manley Hall's work—and, of course, most of them accepted the concept of reincarnation. But that was not the only reason for the subject's interest; he said he had occasional flashes of scenes he could not really have remembered. Beyond that, he admitted much of his life had a cycle of getting hurt (physically or psychologically), looking for answers, getting hurt again. Was there some reason for it, some purpose to what was happening? He hoped that searching the past would help. The doctor agreed to ask some of the questions the subject wanted answered, as well as his own.

He seemed level-headed, mentioned he taught a men's Sunday school class back home in Pennsylvania, and had joined the A.R.E. because of his interest in Edgar Cayce's readings on the Bible, particularly the Book of Revelation. The fact that he was a stockbroker, an investment analyst for a Philadelphia firm, indicated that a number of people believed he was worthy of their confidence.

Now as he appeared to sleep on the couch, could they see what was hid inside of him?

The wire recorder was switched on—9:30 p.m., May 22, 1952.

First, Dr. George encouraged his subject to go back to an early childhood happening. Al's adult voice, speaking in childish accents, told how the governess, Lizzie, had spilled something hot on him, in his crib; it went down the front of his dress. (Dress? Certainly. Little Al was in his crib, and tots all wore gowns in bed in the early 1900s.) It seemed that his parents had gone out; Lizzie put him in his crib and fed him the hot soupy stuff, and it spilled. It burned him; he hurt. Bad. More vivid details. Yes, it was obvious that Al had gone back in time. Back to age two, at any rate.

"And now we want you to go back before this, before you

were born. We want you to go back on a trip into the past. Now you can do that. You have that power . . . You have many pleasant memories. Bring these memories up to the surface for us."

The sleepy voice said, "Jack. That was my name, Jack."

"Jack what? Tell us more about Jack. You can bring it up."

"Carstairs." Then, almost as an afterthought, "1845."

"When you were born," murmured the doctor. "Where were you born?"

Unlike the psychologists and psychiatrists doing past-life regressions today for healing purposes, Henry George was primarily interested in gathering verifiable data, as much as he could, and so he asked for numbers, dates, statistical information (which would not always be available to the identity, such as eight-year-old Jack Carstairs, unless an "observer" personality was listening and spoke up.)

Under soft probing, a young boy's phrasing came from the grown man's lips. "Columbus, Ohio. The street . . . 171 Jackson Avenue." His father's name? "Samuel." His mother's? "Ruth."

Asked to tell about his home, the sleeper said, "There was grass. In the front yard was a tree, a maple tree." He described his red-brick school and the teacher's name, Miss Gimbel.

"What did you do when you stopped school?"

The answer was quick, but not the expected teen-ager ready to go to work. The child's tone: "Eight years old, September 1, 1853. Climbing a tree and the second branch broke and I fell."

"Were you hurt?"

"Yeah. I fell about ten feet, onto the grass, on my backside. Didn't hurt too much but I run in bawling. My father put a wet cloth on my head, in the living room." As a youngster who was trying to impress his elders, he added, "The rug was red, it had blue spots on it, in the front room."

This was not the progression from grade school to high school and beyond; it was the eight-year-old's recollection of when he stopped going to school because he got hurt.

"And my father said, 'Jack, you all right?' He was crying. I was hurt."

(A 1983 search of state records in Columbus, Ohio, showed there was indeed a Jackson Street there in 1845. The records also listed a Samuel Carstairs as a Columbus resident.)

But the focus of this first memory was on the child who was hurt, and the love his father showed in comforting him.

The questioning now turned toward historical data. Who was president? "Polk," was the schoolboy's answer. The history book said that James K. Polk was president from 1845, the year of Jack's birth, to 1849—not 1853, the year Jack was eight years old. Polk, however, was the last, until 1853, to serve a full term in office. The next president, Zachary Taylor, died during his first year in office! Millard Fillmore served out the rest of Taylor's term, a fact which would have been of little or no interest to the Ohio farm boy and his family.

Some hypnotists have cautioned that if a person was speaking from a previous lifetime, that didn't necessarily mean he or she was telling the facts. If you were regressed to a person who was not well informed, *when you were in his or her identity,* you would be no better informed than that person was, despite what you knew when not hypnotized. But if you went to a more knowledgeable identity, your answers would be different. Even if what you said as a regressed personality was not accurate according to history, it would be accurate for that personality. Not all of us today are aware of what is going on across the country, and if we were regressed from the future to this period, we would be no wiser than we are now—unless we could see both this life *and* other lives, perhaps from an observer personality or from a dimension between lives.

It is interesting that a Media, Pa., mother who is also a therapist reported that when her five-year-old—who had been terribly disturbed at loud bangs such as fourth-of-July fireworks—was told to relax, close his eyes, and tell what he thought of when he heard the bangs, he spoke with adult knowledge of guns and tents, referring to a life as a soldier in the Civil War.[1]

In his searching for solid facts, Dr. George did not appear to worry about whether he was addressing his questions to Al in the identity and age he had last given or to someone speaking through any part of time—as if he expected to find Al omniscient whenever hypnotized.

Dr. F. L. Marcuse, in his text on hypnosis,[2] indicates that there is usually good rapport between the hypnotist and the subject. Depending on how the question is asked, the subject will try to produce an answer.

So Al answered, when Henry George asked questions which covered a wide time frame; he asked at one point, "Where were you in 1860?—1870?—1880?—1890? each time receiving consistent answers. Al, as Dr. Marcuse suggested, appeared to shift his own time perspective to try to meet the doctor's expectations. It did seem as if an "observer" would often—though not always—supply dates and other information, able to see the present as well as the past, as William James and Jack Hilgard had noted.

As the witnesses listened, Dr. George continued to draw out information about Jack Carstairs's enlisting in the American Civil War, about his father, his father's funeral, his marriage to a Chinese girl, his life in Toronto, working in a mill there, and losing an arm to a saw.

The doctor's questions sometimes took a turn away from the time line. After discussing how his father left Jack title to a house in Toronto, he asked, "Did you like to swim when you were a young man?"

"Loved it."

"Did you teach swimming?"

"I loved to teach swimming. I liked for people to know how to take care of themselves in the water." (In his present life, Al had also been a good swimmer and, beyond that, an instructor for the Red Cross in lifesaving techniques.)

"Did anyone ever drown where you were?"

"I did once, but that was in the previous incarnation."

The doctor picked up immediately on the cue. Al was seeing across life boundaries! "Where was that, do you remember?"

"France." But the overseeing one wanted to get back to Jack in Canada. Jack continued, "I taught swimming in different schools, up in Toronto."

"Could you name one of the schools?"

"Freedland."

It was several minutes later, after questions and answers on friends he had known, horses he owned, the Chinese songs his wife sang, how he liked to play Chopin, and how shocking was the news that Abraham Lincoln was shot, that Jack seemed to be getting upset. Dr. George tried to calm him:

"You relax, now, relax."

"Yes," came the sleepy response.

On a hunch that his subject could be shifting to another period, Dr. George asked, "And what was your name?"

"Pierre. March 29, 1710, I was born. Chatil Court. Name was Pierre."

"What was your father's name?"

"Pierre."

"What was your mother's name?"

"I can't remember."

It was not surprising. A father, particularly in the 1700s, would be called by his own name by friends coming over and by other men; a child would hear his father's name called. A mother was . . . well, a mother. Until recently when divorce and single mothers have become more common, many youngsters knew their mothers only as "Mom" or "Ma" or "Mother."

As the questioning continued, Dr. George began asking not about the child's life and emotions but about history, for verifying data. He asked the five year old, "Did you live in the French Revolution?"

The child replied, "I can't remember." His voice sounded frightened. "I can't remember anything!" like a scolded little boy.

The doctor shifted back to the child's frame of reference.

"Remember the country?"

"Beautiful country. I was killed in an accident. I don't want to remember that. I don't want to remember."

"Can you say a few words as the people spoke there?"

"I don't want to remember," Al repeated, then, "Oh, no!"

(Those two words, though spelled differently in French, "O, non!" would sound almost identical with the English.)

Soothingly, Dr. George urged, "You relax."

Instead of relaxing, Al's body suddenly tensed. The boyish voice called, "Jesus! Jesus!" Then he added, "Appeared in a vision."

The hypnotist repeated, "Appeared to you in a vision?"

"I wish," the boy pleaded. "Couldn't I repeat that vision?" Then, from beyond himself, he knew, "Seventeen fifteen. Five years old." The little Pierre had died.[3]

Then, other identities and other comments came through. Al spoke as a black-robed monk near Naples, answered questions about whether church and state were united, and whether he knew Galileo or Michelangelo. (The friar responded that he had seen Michelangelo working but believed he was not well known at the time.) At the doctor's request, he began to repeat a prayer in Latin, "Laude, laude, Patrem . . . " (Latin for "Praise, praise to the Father . . . ")

A pause and heavy breathing. He sounded disoriented. "I feel like I'm in between somewhere and somewhere else."

"Can you place yourself now?"

"No."

Here the doctor asked a biological question of the in-between-lives personality, "What color are your genes?"

No problem with the answer. A simple, "White."

"Just let yourself relax. You can go back. Tell us what you see?"

To the surprise of questioner and witnesses, Al writhed in discomfort, tried to spit some invisible dirt from his mouth, and protested that the windstorm was blowing sand and dust all around. Achmesh was his name, and he was watching a crucifixion of three men on a distant hill.

In a choked voice, Al described "Three crosses there. All the people are away from it. What are they afraid of? Some woman kneeling at the foot of a cross. Middle, the cross is the middle. He said, 'Father, forgive them, they know not what they do.' And there isn't anything else there. Just a man bleeding. The side of his face is cut. Nails. Look of compassion. 'Father, forgive them,' he said. Quite a distance away but it seems like I'm right up there. I don't see the people any more. It's so beautiful! Can't you see it? It's right over there!"

"What is your tribe?"

"Israel, tribe of Benjamin . . . Don't take me away from that. Storm seems all gone. Seems like, looks like he's dead. But he isn't dead. He's not dead, just smiling . . . A man's coming. Where did all those people go? Where did they go?" He paused as if hoping for an answer, then sighed, "I don't know."

No one wanted to break the silence. The witnesses looked at each other. Four lives. And in one of them the most world-shaking event in two millennia.

3
Clues from the Past

Al could remember. But it was dizzying to remember all the different scenes, the panorama he had passed through in Dr. George's office in just that one May evening.[1] It was almost disorienting to recall so many happenings and feelings that might be distant memories, but seemed as close as yesterday. He had lived the emotions of the Ohio farm boy, his fall from the maple tree, the sweetness of the farm strawberries, the carpentry work, his favorite horse—and it was numbing to realize those were just the latest fragments of . . . whom?

Some of those parts of the past must have felt pain. Perhaps inner pain, the kind he had been trying to escape ever since the death of his baby daughter and his inability to deal with a wife who accepted no explanations. She seemed to want him to feel *her* hell, and he already had enough of his own. It seemed to infuriate her when he went into the bedroom and tried to meditate. Wouldn't it be peace to withdraw from the world? But, of course, he couldn't.

Under the doctor's questioning he had gone far beyond that latest life as Jack Carstairs, 100 years in the past. He'd recalled the fears, then the vision of a little drowning boy, Pierre. And then—with a bit of a shock—he remembered the prayerful isolation of the black-robed priest who actually lived a life withdrawn from the world. Once he had been apart from everything except the Order. There were the brothers, with their own black robes—but most of the time he had seemed to be alone . . . or was that after his parents died in the plague?

Then there had been the incredible sight of the three crosses on the hill. What a horrific sensation, the wind and dirt blowing dreadfully into his eyes, into his mouth. He'd seen the crowds, then felt the silence, the fright, and foreboding.

What would come next? It was hard to get through his work at the investment company, it was hard to make the necessary plans, while he wondered about who else and what else was concealed in his past.

Wordsworth had said, "The child is father of the man . . . " Were these other experiences, these other lives, both beginnings—like a child, each life starting a different existence in geography and in time, and then—like a father, causing other beginnings: each life bringing forth something new, a quality, maybe some cell memory, that was in *him* here and now, his "soul ancestry," the "father" of this middle-aged man who felt adrift in a spiritual sea?

He had thought, when he first approached Dr. George, that if he could just look into his past, he would begin to see a pattern in his present and would know better if he were headed in the right direction, be able to predict his future with some chance of success.

But instead, after that first session, he wasn't really ready to predict a thing! In fact, it felt harder to tell where he ought to be; he felt like a wanderer between worlds—one, the present, the others, *lifetimes.* One hundred, 200, 500, even 2,000 years ago. And those worlds felt real, too.

It would be two weeks before the next session with Dr. George. There was a lot more to this than just knowing he had lived before. He had problems to solve, work to do, and decisions to make. He'd had bouts of depression. Headaches. Physical problems. Not the least of them, he thought as he paused to catch his breath, was his own heart. He had experienced four heart attacks already. Would the kind of excitement he felt when he saw those crosses in that Hebrew life bring on another one? He didn't want to leave this life just when he was about to find out whether it made sense!

One of the primary questions he had asked Dr. George when they had discussed the process after he had first volunteered was whether they could find out if he had strong ties to any religion, to any faith. And in his first session he had recalled the feelings of the lone friar. Prayerful. Withdrawn. Not what he had expected. And about God—he had done so much reading but was convinced now that knowing God was not something you could do with your brain. He sensed that it had to be an inner, emotional knowledge. God was real and strong; the very existence of Gladys proved it! Now, the big question: what did God want him to do?

There had to be a strong tie with the Hebrew man.

Now he knew it wasn't just a whim that had made him offer to teach the men's Bible class. And it wasn't just a recollection of his father as a well-known Methodist layman.

Now, that explosion of memory that had Achmesh writhing, trying to protect himself from the windstorm and swirling dirt while he stood and watched the three men on the hilltop—that explosion gave a whole new feeling to the word *God,* to the word *Father.* Now, even walking around in the bright May sunlight, Al was feeling the chills. He had been close to—he had actually *seen*—someone indescribable. He, at least a part of himself, had been there!—And he wanted to live to go back.

But that was only a part of it. Was he perhaps repeating in this life mistakes he had made before? If so, how was he to learn better? If he had hurt people in his past life or lives, well, he had read about karma, the cosmic balancing which fit that biblical saying, "As ye sow, so shall ye reap." But it was clear from what everyone could observe that the repayment in kind, the returning to a person the kind of things he or she did, good for good, evil for evil, was not really working in *this* world. Some people he knew who had cheated were living well and happily; some who had slaved and devoted themselves to good works were treated miserably.

The Hindus thought that your errors in one lifetime would bring you to some kind of disgrace in the next, some lowering, punishment, humiliation. But good deeds would raise you. If you did well as a laborer and servant, in your next life you might be a leader, a lord. And perhaps, looking at past lives as Dr. George was enabling him to do, he might later be able to know where he stood, what the score was. How much did he still owe? What would he have to pay?

He wrote to Gladys, "I know I feel so much closer to understanding God's love when I think about you," then he tried to put from his mind the ironic possibility that his physical problem might cut off his search for the spiritual goal; he might die before getting there.

"Getting there" also applied to Virginia Beach. He had asked Gladys to be his wife—and she had agreed. But there was no way she would agree to leaving her work with the A.R.E.; she made it clear that working with the Edgar Cayce readings was an integral part of her life, ever since she first started working for Mr. Cayce in 1919, nearly thirty-three years ago. Consequently, *he* would have to move from his apartment near Philadelphia and would have to transfer his work to Virginia Beach. But he wouldn't mind. There was something about that place that made it easier to talk about spiritual matters. One of the very few places where it was comfortable to talk about them. That was something he had to do. The transition would take a few months. Meanwhile, he would commute to work each week.

Al told the people at Auchinchloss, Parker, and Redpath that he would be leaving within six months.

Dr. Henry George was not a psychiatrist, but an osteopathic physician and hypnotist. With his patients his primary interest was their health; with the volunteers for his regression study, the primary interest was not so much in healing or solving their problems but in attempting to probe their past-life recall and to search for data and documentation that would "prove" they had lived before.

Before the second session, Dr. George reviewed the typist's transcript of the first. In appreciation for his volunteers—who, of course, were not paid—he had agreed to include among his questions any topics in which they were especially interested. Al had mentioned an interest in religion and religious types of organizations. Jack Carstairs, the doctor noted, had mentioned it *before* he went into the army. Yes. And there were other clues.

The Carstairs family had moved northward to Cleveland. By 1860, at age fifteen, Jack did help his father as a carpenter, but then left the farm. Where did he go?

"Went to school again," he had said.

"What did you study this time?"

"Something about a minister."

"You became a minister?"

"No. Studied to be one. Stopped. Didn't like it."

There had been an interesting shift on page 6. "Jack" was describing his enlistment and battles, and then somehow found himself in a church. Was there a connection? He read on.

"And then what did you do?"

"I went into the army against the confederates. I thought that was the thing to do."

"What regiment were you in?"

"Down at Bull Run . . . 31st regiment."

"For what state?"

"Illinois. I went to Illinois from Ohio and enlisted."

"You were in the Battle of Bull Run?"

"Wounded in the arm."

"Which arm?"

"Left arm. In the upper muscle," he said, and as the doctor asked how he was treated, Jack described being taken to a field hospital, a tent.

"And how did they treat the wound?"

"They took alcohol and washed it. It wasn't bad."

"And did they release you out of the army then?"

"No, I was at Manassas."

The doctor had asked whether he was injured at Manassas, but Al seemed to be slipping away.

"Something about a church," Al murmured.

"You see a church? Was this on the battlefield?"

"No. Big steeple. In Richmond. On Spicer Street. I was in the church."[2]

Asked for the time and date, Al murmured, "Three o'clock in the afternoon. It was Sunday . . . 31st of July, 1864."

"And what happened?"

"A funeral of some kind . . . "

"Look into the casket and tell us who it was."

There was a pause, then Al answered, "My father, Samuel."

Silence, and a sense of grief. Was this juxtaposition of the wounding, the church, and his father's funeral connected to the religious theme? Because of the visible sadness, Doctor George had urged Al, "And now pass on to happier experiences. Tell us more about Jack."

"That's my name, Jack." So at this point Al *was* Jack. But he went on, "I don't have any use for it—for women."[3]

"Why don't you have any use for women? Did they hurt you?"

"No. I just think there is something more to life. There must be."

"What more is there?" Yes, it was a strange question to ask the farm boy turned soldier, but it had opened a new aspect on the major theme when followed by, "What was your aspiration?"

"To commune with God."

"And how did you want to obtain this?"

"Study to show thyself approved . . . A workman is not to be ashamed . . . "

Portions of Bible verses a workman would find appropriate. Study—he had studied, obviously. And the next questions the doctor asked would show an interesting twist to the studies.

"Bring up in your memory those people that influenced your life during your religious study." (No time period mentioned.)

"Cardinal . . . something. I can't remember."

"Was he a Catholic?"

"I wasn't, but he was."

(Apparently Dr. George was unaware that the only church which has cardinals is the Catholic church.)

Al described going to see this American cardinal in Boston: "A kind man, lovely, peaceful. I wanted to find out what he had to teach me."

"And did you find out?"

"He made me a Catholic."

"A priest?"

"No, just a Catholic. I studied and studied, but I didn't think I could become a priest. I wasn't good enough."

Jack seemed to believe others knew more than he did. Dr. George reflected that Al had not seemed to feel at all inferior when in the life of the priest. If he were a psychologist instead of an osteopath, he might work with that.

"What did you study? Could you tell us some of the books?"

"A red book it was." Then Al murmured the name, "Valzack," and paused, seeming puzzled.

"*He* wasn't Catholic. How did I get ahold of that thing? Somehow or other. Maybe that's why I stopped being a Catholic."

Could there have been two red books, one given him by the Cardinal and another red one by—the doctor could think of no author named "Valzack." No "Valzack" in the 1860s or '70s who could have written such a book. But—wasn't there a writer named Balzac? A quick search in his references and yes, Honoré de *Balzac* had indeed come to prominence as a writer by 1850 and was known both for his collection of romance novels and his cuttingly realistic *Human Comedy!* (It would be five years later, 1957, when that popular show, *The Music Man*, appeared on Broadway, the show in which the town mayor's haughty wife condemns the reading of "dirty books" by Rabelais and "Baaalzac!") Yes, a translation of Balzac might well turn a reader from Catholicism.

The visit with the Cardinal had to be later in Jack's life. The doctor had tried a question to learn about his middle age:

"Now suppose we come to the time ten years before your death. Think back and tell us where you were."

Here, as in other times when asked to look over a long period of his life, Jack was quick with dates and figures—

trying to please the hypnotist and give him everything he wanted:

"I was fifty-three when I died and that makes me forty-three. I was in Toronto, Canada, working in a mill there. Carpenter. Boss's name . . . what was it? What was the name of the mill?" Jack seemed to have the same irritation at forgetting those formerly familiar names as most folks past their prime have with labels that once leaped to their lips.

"You were living in Toronto and you were working in a mill?"

"Lost my arm," Al had muttered. "Saw cut my arm off."

"Which arm was it?"

"Right arm . . . Hurts."

"And you were treated in a hospital or a doctor's home?"

"Toronto General Hospital."

Going after data, Henry George next asked, "Do you remember the doctor?"

Without hesitation, "Dr. Stevens."

"Do you remember what year?"

"1885."

"And did the loss of your right arm have a profound effect upon you?"

"I didn't want to work any more." This time the voice sounded depressed. Asked what he did then, he answered briefly, "I studied."

"And what did you study?"

"Bible."

This was the time to ask another question Al had previously requested. "Did you believe in reincarnation?"

"No." No hesitation at all. "That's right. That (reincarnation)'s rubbish. I don't believe in that stuff."

The witnesses looked at each other. One was tempted to say, "Look who's talking."

The doctor continued: "Did the Catholic priest condone your reading the Bible?"

"I didn't let him know it."

After his father's death Jack had said that his aspiration was "to commune with God." Dr. George asked him, at this point some thirty years later, "What was your goal in life then?"

"Union with God," was the answer. Jack added, "See, I didn't see it in church, in any church. I saw it . . . " His voice trailed off.

This seemed to be a good time to ask questions Al had wanted about affiliations with special groups or orders with religious implications. In his present life, his father had been a Mason, his brother Brinkley a Mason, and he, Al, had joined the Rosicrucians. To the question, "Did you belong to any clubs at that time? Were you a Mason?" the short but definite answer to both was, "No."

Something else they had to clear up. "Were you married at this time?"

"I was married, yes."

His wife's name was Sara, and they lived in Toronto. He gave the house number and street: Belle Street, 15."[4]

Asked if he had any children, Jack answered, "No." He was then in his fifties. There were no children in the home in 1895. The doctor had put the question without making it clear whether he was referring just to this time or to the whole married life.

But Henry George wondered if Sara had any effect on Jack's beliefs.

"And where did she come from?"

"She came from Philadelphia."

Asked if her parents were Dutch, Jack said they were Chinese.

"What was her religion?"

"She didn't have any." Interesting.

Dr. George had noted in Jack Carstairs's account some items he might use for his own search for "proof" that this man had lived when and where he said. But following it up would take a great deal more time. At least the hypnotist had found clues in the pattern seen in the life as Jack Carstairs which would have special meaning to his volunteer. Al had been seeking a spiritual path, had tried to study for the ministry, but gave it up. He was not successful as a student. Small wonder, since he had left school when he was eight years old. His vocabulary had been simple, not the full expressions Albert Turner could use. The doctor sighed. This search for meaning was the prime reason why Al had volunteered to be a subject, but not why Dr. George had accepted him. The understanding was, they would cooperate.

Of course, Al still had a living to make. But it was as if the present days seemed scanty and the past seemed rich. Not rich in the sense of money, but in the significance, in the possible connections to an indefinable power.

He could still work with investments when he moved to Virginia Beach. Or, since he loved plants—come to think of it, Jack Carstairs loved plants, growing things on the farm, didn't he?—Al might get a greenhouse, grow plants, grow fig trees, grow gardenias!

Gladys was glad to have him move to Virginia Beach. But she was not happy about his continuing to be a volunteer in Dr. George's quest for past lives.

"Edgar Cayce found out about people's past lives," Al pointed out. "He often gave readings about them."

"But," Gladys would say, "Edgar Cayce put *himself* in a trance, for those life readings." She was uneasy. You couldn't tell what frequent hypnosis would do.

Al tried to reassure her. Gladys knew Henry George was a doctor of osteopathy and was aware that Edgar Cayce in a trance had recommended him to a client—that Dr. George had later come to see Mr. Cayce and been friendly. The doctor had first thought he might be a "con man," as psychologist Harmon Bro had once feared. But Dr. Bro was now a staunch ally of the A.R.E., and Dr. George was as well. Still, Gladys couldn't help worrying about the prolonged use of hypnotic states.

Dates and places had already been set for the second and third sessions, at the Philadelphia home of a woman physician, who was one of the intrigued witnesses of the first session. The fourth session would not be until June 29. With input from Gladys Davis and Hugh Lynn Cayce, they had arranged for it to be held at the A.R.E. headquarters in Virginia Beach. At that time, Gladys could attend, too, and see for herself what exactly was going on. After that, she would not be able to object.

4

Probing the 1800s

An alert, petite, and sparkling woman of ninety-eight, Mrs. Hadassah Roberts moved to her chair with the aid of a walker. At her home in Arden, Delaware, in September of 1993, she cheerfully discussed her own experiences with Dr. Henry George forty-one years before in 1952, when she was a young fifty-seven.

"Henry George was trying to *prove* reincarnation—that we had lived life after life—and to trace the important factors in our lives. Several of us were in the Theosophical Society and took part in some of his sessions. He hoped the Society would use the recordings he had made, but they were not especially interested in keeping them.

"I remember Morey Bernstein worked with Dr. George and with the group several times. Dr. George wasn't happy when Morey Bernstein's book, *The Search for Bridey*

Murphy, came out just four years later, and he didn't have one written.

"Our group took turns being the subjects. I was regressed several times. I remember three different lives—in one, in the early 1800s, I was a male, in Burlington, N.J. I had three sisters. Then in the next life," she said with a laugh, "one of them was my wife!"

Some of the influences from previous lives affected this life, she had found. For one example: because she drank a lot in two previous lives, with unpleasant consequences, she detested alcohol in this one. Dr. George had also noticed connections like that in other regressions he had handled.

Hadassah Roberts was also a witness at several sessions, including one with Albert Turner as subject. "Henry George would hold a bright object up (like a gold watch on the end of a chain) and swing it like a pendulum while he talked softly, and you'd lie back on the couch and watch. It worked quickly."

Al found his way to the second session, which was not in Wilmington but in Philadelphia, at the home of a red-haired woman physician. Shortly after he lay down and received the introductory directions, he responded as Jack Carstairs:

"I was in New York. Horses. On Canal Street, 45 Canal Street. Everybody was losing money. I finally sold the horses—three black horses."

"Who did you sell them to?"

"A red-faced man. His name was Smith, Lausch. That was his business. He paid me $50 apiece. I would have gotten $150 if it wasn't for the panic, April 2nd, 1872.[1] I sold the horses. (Added sadly:) I loved horses."

A love of horses was something Jack carried from his childhood; whenever he spoke of them, it was with affection. In his childhood period, asked what he wanted to grow up to be, he said plainly, "Just wanted to ride horses. Like the Wild West and all. Talk about the gold rush and everybody going out west with the horses and hitching the wagon up. I wanted to go out west and ride horses!"

"Did you go?" Henry George had asked.

"No. Stayed home and went to school." A sigh.

"Now, tell us some happy memories you have. Some other memories you had there."

A boyish laugh. "Ha! The first cow I saw was funny. Moo! I didn't know what it was, and I ran," he admitted, explaining from an older eight-year-old view. "I was five years old. Everybody come, thought something happened to me, but I was just scared of the cow; I didn't know what it was." An eight-year-old, of course, was much wiser.

"How much land did your farm have?" Ten acres was the answer. "Did you have a wood lot on it? Were there trees growing on it?"

"Let me see. Yeah," he replied thoughtfully. "There was sort of a hillock, it wasn't a hill, in front of some kind of trees, big, tall trees. There wasn't much of a woods, maybe an acre, that's all."

The doctor suggested he go further on and recall when he enlisted in the army. Jack confirmed that he had enlisted at Decatur, Illinois, on March 2, 1860, in the 31st regiment. This was at 141 Bonn Street, he volunteered. "That's where I went in the front door and they gave me gray pants, a blue coat, buttons on it, a funny-looking hat, street car conductor or something," he said—as if he was observing this from the viewpoint of the eight-year-old who had answered the earlier questions.

"What kind of emblem was on the cap?" the doctor wanted to know. "Examine the cap closely."

Jack replied, as a fifteen year old, "It had an arrow pointing downwards through the emblem, 'In Union There Is Strength,' in gold letters; wasn't gold, but it looked like gold, on sort of a copper background in a circle, and the arrow was with a feather on top of it pointing downwards. The cap was blue, with gray lid. I was fifteen years old, and I went in as a drummer boy, 31st regiment."

"What was your name?" Sometimes the doctor would question as if to catch him in an identity shift.

"Carstairs. *Private* Jack Carstairs."

"And you were a drummer?"

"A drummer boy," Jack corrected. "I could drum good, too!"

"And where did your regiment go from Decatur?"

"Gettysburg, Pa. We trained there."

The doctor encouraged him to go on.

"That's right, big field. I used to play the drums for marching."

Seeking more data to verify, he switched back and asked: "Now tell me about your Civil War experience. What happened in 1862?"

"Wounded."

"Where were you wounded?"

"Battle of Bull Run. I'll tell you how it happened. It was a hill. There was a sniper on top. Wasn't very far away. A graze wound. Nothing heroic about that." Jack seemed anxious to avoid any appearance of bragging.

Dr. George asked again what regiment he was in, and Al repeated what he had given in the first session: the 31st Illinois Regiment. He was in "A" Company. Infantry. This time, Al also recalled another officer's name: Pete Rice.

Next came other potentially verifiable questions: "What kind of gun did you use?"

"Began with a 'G'—Grand Rapids,[2] I think it was."

"How many shots did it shoot at one time?"

"One. Had to reload."

"How did you reload it?"

"Powder."

"Was it a separate cartridge and ball, or all in one casing?"

"All in one casing."

That gave them some information they could check.

In a later session, the fourth, at Virginia Beach, once again "Jack Carstairs" was back in battle, repeating what he had said before but adding several details. "I liked to ride horses, but they put me in the infantry. Fifteen years old, a drummer boy. I went to Gettysburg for training and they transferred me to Company A." He had been in both the first and the second Battle of Bull Run. He gave a more graphic description of the wound in the arm and wondered aloud why they seemed excited about it when it "wasn't a bad wound," but they sent him home.

Jack added a part he played in the siege of Richmond in 1863. "I was sent ahead of the army. There was a lot of excitement. I'm in Richmond. I was sent ahead to explore the fortifications as a civilian. My name was given as Samuel Houston for that purpose.[3] A great deal of commotion. I had to slip back to Captain Grant"—not General Grant, he explained, but Captain Fred Grant—"he was lieutenant of my company, but he was captain at this time, and I told him what I saw."

"What did you see?"

Although he protested that it would take too long, Jack nevertheless filled in the story of how he discovered a trap that was laid on Vivian Street. He found that "dynamite was set to be exploded, at an intersection at the corner of Vivian and Bolt Streets, if the Union armies came there." This was the kind of adventure a young soldier would enjoy telling later on, more than the blood and guts and woundings.

The doctor decided to leave the war scenes for the time being and review family information. He confirmed that the Chinese girl Jack Carstairs married was named Ming, but he had changed it to Sara "so people would like her better." She had come with her parents from Shanghai; they were married in Philadelphia, when they were both fifteen.

Jack seemed to enjoy talking about his wife and said she was the best thing that happened to him, the happiest experience he had. Although he was in the army when they married, he came home as often as he could. He did feel a little guilt about how he treated her. Sara wanted to wear Chinese clothes, but Jack "made her dress as an American" and admitted regretfully, "That wasn't right." He moved with her to Toronto because people accepted her better there. Still he traveled frequently between Philadelphia and Toronto, even during the war.

The doctor asked again, "Did you have any children?"

"Yes, two children, Bob and Alice." (Unlike the last time Dr. George had asked the question, when Jack was over fifty, this time he had just been speaking about an earlier period. This time, he said yes.)

"Where was Bob born?"

"Philadelphia, Pennsylvania." Asked for the date, he said, "December 1, 1869. Robert Earl Carstairs."[4]

"And where was Alice born?"

"In Toronto. Alice . . . She died at birth." (We do not know if Al ever saw a connection between losing the daughter, Alice, and losing a three-day-old daughter in his present life.)

At first Dr. George seemed to have missed that last part. He continued, "Did your wife take good care of them? How did she treat them as children?"

"Very, very good. She was sweet."

"Did she sing to them?" Then he realized there was only one living child. "Did she sing to Bob?"

"Yes."

"What kind of songs did she sing?"

"Chinese lullabies."

Asked to give the tune of one of these songs, Jack sang a series of syllables, up and down four notes of the scale, in a rhythmic pattern. Were there other songs? There were a lot of them, but he didn't remember enough to sing them, he explained.

Jack did recall that he loved to play music on the piano. "Anything Chopin. Loved Chopin, étude 37."

"Do you remember it now?"

Jack hummed some of it. But when Dr. George asked if he would like to play it later, Jack first protested, "I don't have any place to play it."

Apparently the hostess did have a piano, for Dr. George continued, "Would it make you feel better if you could get to a piano and play that piece? Think of how you felt then. Would you like to have a piano before you?"

"No," came the prompt answer. "It's some memories I don't want."

It seemed that the command, "Think of how you felt then," had triggered recall of something Jack could not or would not face. Puzzled, Henry George asked, "They are unpleasant memories?"

"That's right."

Some part of Jack recoiled from those memories; they were enough to cut off the desire for Chopin. But Dr. George still wanted a demonstration of the music. He asked a new question.

That question might have brought a different answer if the doctor had asked only the first part, "What other pieces did you like?" but he added, "What other music did you like?"

The man on the couch answered the last part, "I had an organ down in Richmond, sort of a funny kind of organ, pedals and pump . . . A little organ with two keyboards, one above the other, three octaves on the upper keyboard and five on the lower keyboard. I bought it off a church. I don't know why they wanted to get rid of it. Nice ol' thing, and I used to play it all the time."

Jack obviously had enjoyed playing on the little pump instrument. Dr. George went on: "Do you recall the last time you played on the organ?"

Here again, music and time and emotions made a strong and triple connection. A connection with an event Jack was refusing to face. While Al was in the trance, the observer part of him was speaking up to prevent his getting hurt from memories too anguishing for him to handle.

"I don't want to talk about that."

But the doctor probed, "Do you remember the year?"

Jack Carstairs would not be led back to that experience. He tried to change to something he *did* like to talk about: "Somebody gave me a pretty bridle. Sort of brass and copper, for the horse, Gal. She likes it, too . . . " He corrected himself quickly: "*He* likes it, it's a him, not a her." His favorite horse he called "Gal" even though it was male. "I guess because he was sort of sweet. He used to look at me with those big, brown eyes." The witnesses had to smile at that. "Gal" brought happy memories, and those were available for answers.

But the doctor, perhaps on purpose, had not appeared to recognize the switch. "When did you play that?" he said.

Again Jack refused to return to the music subject, but since the doctor had asked "when" meaning "a date," he gave a date—but of something entirely different: "1892 in March. Snowstorm."

Now Henry George understood that Jack had left the music topic altogether. He might as well go along. "And where were you then?"

"Toronto."

"Do you remember any of the papers or magazines?"

"*Toronto General Star* . . . That's the one I used to read every day."

Going after more data, Henry George asked about school and home; he was told that Bob went to school in Philadelphia, and their Philadelphia home was at 1212 Spring Garden Street. (Another time Jack gave the address as 2012, which is still a row house today.)

"Then we moved back to Toronto, to Bleeker Street—172." (There is a Bleeker Street in Toronto.) Then Bob went to school there. "Sister Annie. A Catholic school."

"Did you always live in the same house?"

"No, I moved twice."

"Will you give us the addresses of your other homes? Did you own your home?" (Here again the hypnotist asked two questions together. The subject answered the last one first.)

"It cost $15,000 to own it. I inherited it from my father, because I didn't make that much. This was Delancey Place—15 Delancey Place, Toronto."

(Although there is no Delancey Place in Toronto at present, there IS a *Delano* Place. It is possible he mixed Delancey Place in Philadelphia with Delano Place in Toronto.)

Looking for other details, the questioner asked again about the boy, Robert. "Did Bob go to school? Where?"

"Yeah . . . in Philadelphia."

Jack explained that Bob started school in 1876 when he was about seven years old. He later continued at a Catholic school in Toronto.

To round out the travels, the doctor asked, "Did you come back into this country after 1890—the U.S., that is?"

"Lots of times," Jack answered quickly. "Buffalo. I used to have a girl there." He added, in a penitent tone, "Shouldn't do that because I was married."

Asked for her name, he said, "Louise," then protested, "I don't want to talk about that. Shouldn't do that. That's not right."

To calm him, the doctor tried shifting the subject. "What else did you do?"

But Jack was wound up. "That's not right, that's not right."

"You were working in Toronto?"

This time the subject shifted successfully. "Toronto, Canada. I liked it up there. Pretty."

Later, the doctor asked, "Was your wife always faithful to you?" This triggered another series of apologetic protests.

"No. That's why I went to see Louise, but that was no excuse. No excuse at all. It doesn't excuse me at all." (In his present life, rumors said that Al, when teaching lifesaving classes during the early days of WWII, had done more than casual flirting with some of the volunteers.)

Dr. George wanted to find the limits of Jack Carstairs's life and the consistency of his memory:

"Tell me where you were living in 1850."

"Columbus, Ohio."

"And in 1860?"

"Two places. I was in Richmond and I was in Toronto."

"And in 1870?"

"Toronto."

"And in 1880?"

"Toronto."

"And in 1890?"

"I was in Boston, and I also lived in Toronto."

So far, the memories of dates and places were consistent with what Jack had said in the first session. He did add later that he often traveled back and forth from Philadelphia to Toronto, and "never seemed to settle down." With the years and places given so surely, without hesitation, he seemed to be speaking from the observer's view.

"In 1900?"

The answer was mumbled. Sounded like, "I was on Venus." The doctor left that answer alone and continued.

"Do you remember where you were in 1895?"

"Here I passed on."

"Can you recall that? If it is unpleasant, you don't have to dwell on it. Can you tell us where you were then?"

"The window. Pneumonia. I'm lying beside the window. My wife is sitting by the bedside. Sara. All of a sudden there is an angel, and just—I walked off. That wasn't unpleasant. It was pleasant."

"Can you give us the date when you 'walked off' "?

"April second, same date just twenty-three years later." (It was the same day of the month he had mentioned in the beginning of the session, April second, the financial panic.) "Veasey St., 4025 Veasey St., Toronto," he added.

That description of just seeing an angel and leaving—out the window or by another exit—is a common report for those describing a near-death experience. One young woman at a meeting of Delaware Valley Near-Death Studies told how she had been badly injured from a motorcycle accident, was lying in her bed, saw "an angel on the ceiling," then went out toward a heavenly light.

Henry George did not continue to explore the pleasant "walking-off" experience.

Jack Carstairs's life was to come up in each of the first four sessions. Dr. George wanted to be able to check addresses, dates, and events he had laboriously drawn from the sleeping subject. That was *his* goal. If Al got answers to some of his philosophical questions, so much the better. Al, meanwhile, had learned that Jack's life had included plenty of stress, frustrations in searching for spiritual direction, and some really pleasant experiences—such as his horses . . . and his wife . . . and his death.

5
James Who?

It was halfway through the evening of June 5, after the obligatory research questions on the most recent life, that Henry George decided to explore further and see if someone new would turn up in Al's past. After all, there were only twenty-two years between Jack Carstairs's death in Toronto and Al's birth in Philadelphia; there were 135 years between the birth of Jack Carstairs in 1845 and the little Pierre in 1710, but over 200 years between Pierre and the priest in 1450. Might there be another personality in there somewhere?

But from what he knew of history, Dr. George had to be disappointed in what the time-traveler came up with next. Al had earlier expressed a belief that he might have lived in England at one time, so the doctor led him there:

"Would you like to go back to one of your previous lives? When did you live in England?"

No answer.

"Who was king when you were in England?"

"James," he said without hesitation.

"What James?"

"James I." He paused, then, "Wait a minute." He spoke as if in a fog. "1585. My name," he hesitated, sighed, " . . . some relation there." He sighed again, as if making a decision. "James II. I was James II, the son . . . of James I. I grew up. Fifteen years old . . . I didn't like it. I went over to France."[1]

The doctor couldn't believe this. "What was your name?"

The sleeper repeated it. The doctor asked again, incredulous, "Your name was *James II?*"

"That's right, James I was king."

Still disbelieving, "You were his son?"

"That's right."

"Who was your mother?"

"Elizabeth."

Now Dr. George was certain this had to be fantasy. How could it be true? Elizabeth had been the queen of England—from 1558 until 1603. There was no way "the virgin queen" could have been the mother of James II. Henry George wasn't on the most intimate terms with English nobility, but he did know that Elizabeth was James I's aunt. Mary, James I's mother, was in fact the half-sister of Elizabeth. A quick look at the encyclopedia gave the parents of James I of England as Mary, Queen of Scots, and Lord Darnley. James I's son was named Charles, not James. If this character's father was James I, he could not be James II. When the first James was born to Mary, in 1566, he was in line for the *Scottish* throne. He was named James VI of Scotland when he was just one year old, in 1567. A regent ruled Scotland for him. It was not until Elizabeth stepped down in 1603 that he was named James I of England as well.

Now, what else could the listeners think—except that the man in the trance was going far over the edge with this wild tale? Playing an imposter? Weren't people in a trance supposed to tell the truth?

Later searching turned up several pieces of related information that threw a different light on the question. For example, the impossibility, as they thought, of his mother being "Elizabeth." Just consider the very human tendency to name a baby after someone famous. After Diana married Prince Charles, a number of babies were christened Diana; Arlene Francis was a movie and TV personality in the '50s; there were many little Arlene Francises in those years. Al's father was an example: named Albert Edward Turner—after Albert Edward, the Prince of Wales and Queen Victoria's husband. After Queen Elizabeth's coronation in 1558, a great many baby girls would be named Elizabeth—the name meant, in Hebrew, "as God is my oath"—in hopes of bringing good fortune to the child. So when James I reached his teens, there was no lack of nubile ladies bearing the name of his aunt, "the virgin queen," the most prominent of all of England's queens to that date (and perhaps since).

For another, the queen had been godmother of all of the children that James I had later by Anne of Denmark!

The son of the Queen of Scots, the royal James had experienced a constricted and unhappy childhood without his mother. Mary was imprisoned when he was but a year old, and he never saw her again. James was reared under stern Scottish tutors. When he reached his active teens, this grandson of Henry VIII was swept into a whirlpool of emotional and political crises. At fourteen, he formed a fast friendship with a handsome youth from France (Esme Stuart, who came to Scotland as an emissary from Mary's French relations and naturally was Catholic). However, as this friendship was ripening, in 1582 James I was kidnapped by ultra-Protestant Scots as a victim of hot religious politics. Forced by the kidnappers to exile his friend from France, the distraught James was later rescued from captivity and in 1583 at seventeen he was able to take on the governing of Scotland—and able to visit England and to have a little fun on his own, for a change. In fact, he gained a reputation for drinking and wenching.[2]

The young man who was James VI of Scotland and shortly to be James I of England had ample opportunity in 1583 and 1584 to be a father if he so wished. The history books do not say that he did, but if he did, it is nice to read that he was later known for his propensity for bringing new young people into the court. His grandfather, Henry VIII, also brought a number of young people in with the last name *Fitzroy,* at court, according to S. C. Antholz, a Tudor researcher. (Fitz = "son of"; Roy = *roi,* French for "king")

Of course, James I had to have a proper marriage, and in 1589 asked for the hand of the fourteen-year-old Princess Anne of Denmark (who came with a handsome dowry). He went to meet the princess, who was marooned by the snow in Norway on her way to England, and they were married there. Afterward, according to a contemporary, "he drank stoutly till springtime." Of their seven children, none was named James, and only three survived to be adults. Therefore, no *legal* son of James I was James II.

England did, of course, have a perfectly legal James II, but this was two generations later, in 1685. This James succeeded his brother, Charles II, son of Charles I, and *grandson* of James I. This James II was driven from the throne by a "bloodless revolution" in 1688.

Could there be a connection in the names, this so-called "James II" as an incarnation of Al, unrecorded but fitting the dates given and the opportunities, and the James II two generations later, as well?

In one of the readings given by Edgar Cayce on his own previous lives, it seems that Gladys Davis was then a young woman in the court of Louis XIV—and, in fact, his daughter—given a cloistered upbringing. She met the second

James, when he was Duke of York, and "became betrothed," the reading said, but never married because of "political influences and conditions."[3]

W. H. Church, who chronicled many of the readings giving previous lives of the seer, Edgar Cayce, in *Many Happy Returns*[4] cites readings saying that this clandestine union resulted in a son, a "love child," and the hapless young mother was banned from the court. That "love child" was one of the lives of the seer himself. The mother went into a convent, and the child was brought up by a religious order. (We wonder about the possibility of their crossing paths with the other "James" some 300 years later.)

In this and all the following questioning for his English life, Al spoke calmly, politely, in a well-bred manner. He did not descend to the pleading or the fearfulness of Pierre or the casual comments of Jack Carstairs. It seemed, in comparison to the others, to be the most "gentlemanly" of his experiences—which would fit the role of a careful man at court. Perhaps a "James Fitzroy" who knew that he was James I's son, knew that he was illegitimate, but thought this questioning stranger might not know and could believe he was the legitimate James II.

The disheartened hypnotist wondered what he was dealing with, but he did not quit. He asked, "Who was the High Priest of England?"

"High Priest of what?"

A sensible question, from the identity of the man claiming to be James I's son. The head of England *was* the head of the church at that time. The English had a strong Protestant influence, not only from Henry VIII's break with the Catholic church, but from the residual resentment that the Roman church had supported Mary against Elizabeth.

"Of the church," Dr. George said shortly.

Puzzled, "James" asked, "Catholic church?" For this whole period was marked by great tensions between the

Catholic church and the Church of England.

"Of England," the hypnotist clarified.

The answerer muttered, "Church of England . . . Anglican bishop—Rhoades." Then he spelled the name.

Brief research turned up no bishop of that name. "Anglican bishop" was, of course, a correct title. But possibly a title to humor the questioner, since the king (or queen) did head the church at this time. Still, England was in the throes of a religious whirlpool. Elizabeth not long before had dismissed all but one of her sister's bishops and a thousand clergy. Puritans were coming to the fore. Catholics were unhappy, too. Pope Pius V had excommunicated Elizabeth. England still remembered "Bloody Mary's" killing of four bishops, a former archbishop, at least 300 Protestants tortured and slain; then there was Queen Elizabeth's trying and executing some 150 Catholics for treason. This period was not the safest to answer questions about prominent men's religious titles.

Now, Frank Melson took a turn at questioning, pursuing another trail. "Who were you with in France?"

"There was a girl . . . I was fifteen years old." He sighed long and deeply. "I can't get it . . . Carmel in France, just like in Palestine, Carmel in France. So beautiful. And she was fifteen." Al's voice lowered to a whisper. "I better not go on."

"Did your father know you were in France?"

"No. He didn't know then, but he found out and made me come back."

"How did you manage to get away?"

Like a tired man with an emotional memory, the sleeper said very softly, "We had a son—We had a son and then he called me back. On a boat. He took me. I was disguised, nobody knew where I was, I went over and hid, I wandered around the countryside, saw the Tuilleries for awhile, then went through . . . (something that sounded like the French for *Sans S'en Froid* or *Son Son Fron*)—then finally went to this Carmel, to this girl. We had a son."

"What was the son's name?"

"Alan. A-L-A-N." His whisper was barely audible.

"Did he live?"

"He lived."

"In France?"

"That's right. He lived in France and . . . Matron was my wife's name."

"James" had not had the same education James I had, and Matron is not usually considered a French name. Today we consider it almost a generic title. But *Webster's New World Dictionary* says it comes from Middle English and Old French *matrone*, Latin *matrona*, and its primary meaning is "a married woman, a wife (or widow), especially one who has had children"—the perfect title for the woman "James" had to leave behind. And "James" could be discreet. It was not wise to mention some women's names.

Softly James continued, "We weren't married, though . . . and that wasn't right either . . . and she left the boy with monks and she went into a monastery." He sighed, "I went back to England. My father made me come back. I was . . . " Pain showed in his voice. "I don't feel so good now."

Henry George soothed him. "You will feel well, you will feel well." He sighed and seemed to relax.

A couple of questions to ponder.

Why did he use the word Carmel? There was no Carmel listed among French towns on the library atlas. But "Carme" in the modern French dictionary is listed as "shortened from 'Carmel' in the seventeenth century" and the time of "James." It refers to the Carmelites, a religious order with old roots at Mt. Carmel in Palestine, which sprouted branches in Spain and France. The order was opened to women from the thirteenth century onward, with convents for cloistered nuns to lead a life of poverty and prayer, but also for active religious groups. It would make perfect sense for the English youth to describe the tragedy as he did; to him, any religious retreat would be a monastery. He had grown up with no Catholic training, in fact, in an anti-Catholic atmosphere, and his voice held the heartbreak that the mother of his child was in a religious home, and the child—Alan, a good Scottish name—had been placed in another home.

Why did his father make him come home? It was not all peace among England, France, and Spain, as it is now. If both young people were fifteen, "James" could have come over to France around 1600. The Spanish Armada had sailed toward England in 1588, and in the ensuing turmoil a great many rules were broken. But with the defeat of the Armada England broke out in a frenzy of patriotic excitement, which did not die down with other sporadic attacks. Spain certainly wasn't trusted now, and France wasn't much better. Even though "James" had some time to enjoy his young love, France was not a suitable place for him. It had to be *back home* for young "James." No wonder he sounded choked up as he muttered, "I don't feel so good now."

Frank Melson went back to the questioning.

"Did you marry when you were in England?"

"No."

"Did you have any children?"

"That child by Matron, Alan. He was raised by the monks. I could never find him! They took him away." (Sounds of sobs on the tape.)

Time to change the kind of questions. "Who were the great scholars in England?"

"Francis Bacon. I knew him. I was only a young kid." (Sir Francis Bacon, philosopher, essayist, statesman, lived from 1561 to 1626.) When Bacon was at the height of his career, "James" would have been a lad of fourteen or so.

"Where was he at that time?"

"Chesterfield." That borough in Derbyshire during the

English Civil War was the scene of a Parliamentarian defeat. "There were a great many . . . " he started to say, then paused, "but I don't feel good."

Dr. George helped the subject relax, so that he could relieve a pain in his arm which had been in a cramped position.

"Thank you, yes," "James" responded. (This identity was most courteous.)

Before they left this man whom the doctor must have thought was fabricating answers, there was one more important thing to find out. The doctor would lead to it gently.

"Do you have any other pleasant memories of England?"

"Uhh-Uhh. I don't like the place. Always didn't like it."

"Do you remember working or having anyone work on the Scriptures?"

"Oh, a lot of people. Hundreds of them. That's why I guess I had the experience with Matron, because when I came back, I just wanted to improve myself. I knew I had done wrong." Here, as he had done when "Jack Carstairs" visited Louise, the hypnotized man expressed regret and guilt because of a relationship with a mistress. Then he spoke proudly. "I had 450 people doing nothing but translation from German to English."

German, indeed!

This could be a gross blunder, enough in itself to dismiss the work of this "James" as not worth recording, some felt. The doctor knew the translation had to be from Hebrew to English for the Old Testament, and Greek to English for the New. Not German to English. However, *The Bible in Its Ancient and English Versions*, edited by H. Wheeler Robinson, gives full details, the name of each of the translators, and lists their instructions—which include closely comparing most available translations and other Bibles "of the learned Tongues, or French, Spanish, German, Italian, etc . . . "[5] so there *could* have been some German used in that way. The so-called *Gutenberg Bible*, the first book to be printed in moveable type, was in Latin, but sometimes considered German because it was produced in Mainz, Germany, some time before 1456.

The actual number of men of learning whom James I had ordered his bishops to gather, in the final count, was "four *and* fifty," as they said in those days, not 450.[6] If "James" said, "Four hundred fifty," not "Four 'nd fifty," he exaggerated the number of translators.

"Did they do this under your command?"

"That's right."

It is probable that he—like "Bridey Murphy"—was building up the importance of *his* job. It would seem more likely that he assisted the translators, saw to their supplies and food; perhaps he might have filled inkwells, sharpened quill pens, and the like. Then he could say to the outsiders that he "oversaw" the translators' work.

Henry George shifted his questioning.

"Who was the admiral of your fleet at this time?"

"James" thought a moment.

"Vick—eroy." He spelled the name. "Admiral James V I C K - E R O Y."

There is no record of an admiral by that name, but interestingly, as he pronounced it, it is a classical Latin sounding-out of V I C E R O Y, the term for the deputy of a king. And James *was* the king's first name. Perhaps this is one of those quirks that Dr. Weiss described as occurring during some hypnotic regressions.

"From what part of England did he come?"

"Village called Sunset (Somerset?) in the northern part of England."

"What kind of ship did you travel in across the channel?"

"On a pretty ship. That was really pretty."

Here Al begins to talk in a different manner, like a young child, as if another personality was answering, perhaps a five- or eight-year-old. He also breathed more heavily, sounding sleepy. This session, as did most of the others, began late—9:30 in the evening.

"Was it a steamship?" (The questioner would like to catch him in an obvious error.)

"No. Wooden ship. Had a lot of people with oars, sails—a pretty ship, ah, it was pretty—prettiest thing I ever saw! The wind carried it over the channel. Pretty ship," the young personality murmured cheerfully.

"Did you like to sail?"

"Mmmm. Loved it."

"Did you do much of it?"

"No, I just worked, worked, worked, worked, worked." The "child" within him vented his frustration.

"What did you work on?"

"Translating the Bible, helping them, helping them . . . Everybody was working."

"Could you read Hebrew?"

"No," "James" admitted, this time as a diffident young man. "I just got the people to do the work, located the scholars." Indeed there had to be plenty of coordination of support and supplies for these scholars, who were working in six committees, at three different headquarters: two at Cambridge, two at Oxford, and two at Westminster.

"Could you speak French in those days?"

"No. I didn't stay over there very long." This question turned his mind to his lost sweetheart in the convent in France. "That was a sad thing. July 15. Didn't know any better." The voice faded off.

His end could have been tragic. But we will never know; we don't even know where or how he died. For reasons we can only imagine, the doctor did not try to call "James" back again.

A gentle young man, caught by circumstances beyond his control and feeling, somehow, that it was his fault. But we wonder if, in the state between lives, would a man *choose* to be a bastard?

If so, this was not the only time Al did it.

6
The Friar and the Prayer

The nights, even the early summer nights, were long between weekends. Long and lonely. Not quite as bad, though, as the worst ones he had spent. Al had felt his life being torn to shreds back when the baby had died and his wife had a depression that kept her hospitalized, ill, and angry; he was laid low with not just stomach troubles but a near-fatal heart attack. Back then, he had wanted to get away from the world, to shut it all out. Go off on his own, to meditate and pray. He could never, would never do that now, because the hypnotist-doctor had shown him that each life is connected to another life. And because, no matter how restful it was, peace—without Gladys—would not be peace.

Living in limbo, without being sure of his path and his goals, had its own stresses. Discussing it with Gladys on Saturday, over cups of tea, he laughed ruefully. "I thought the answers would come out plainly. Find your talents and use them. Do good. Pray to God. If only it were that simple!"

Gladys's musical laugh was sympathetic. "That is why so many thousands of people asked Mr. Cayce for help—because they thought a psychic could just pull answers out of the air, and they could solve their problems without working on themselves."

"I must be making *some* progress," Al grinned and held her hand in his. "I feel happier every time we're together. But these glimpses of previous lives are raising more questions than they're answering."

What had they learned so far? There were tantalizing hints of wonderful spiritual discovery, but he, in whatever guise, had appeared to gain only brief snatches of enlightenment, such as that time with the cardinal in Boston when he was Jack Carstairs; before that, intense but short pain when the drowning French lad had the vision; and that frustration of "James," the guilt-ridden fellow who had to leave his love in a French convent and go home—later to help the Scripture translators.

"I don't seem to be finding what *I* need," he admitted. "But I've told you how I tried—some time back—to become psychic, practicing those exercises, studying those books. If I developed my own psychic ability, maybe I wouldn't have to be hypnotized. Did Edgar Cayce say anything about developing psychic ability?"

Yes, Gladys told him. Several times, in fact. She looked up some of the readings on the subject.

One man had asked, "Are there any exercises you can give me for the development of my faculty of intuition?"

The reply: "Much might be given, but ye are ready for little of same yet. Find first thy relationship to thy Maker." (815-7) For such people, Mr. Cayce had often referred to Deuteronomy 30:11, 19 and its statement that God's word "is not hidden from thee, neither is it far off . . . I have set before you life and death . . . therefore choose . . . "

Al shook his head. "I read the Bible. I've read it from one end to the other. Several times, in fact! Of course, anyone would choose life. But life *after* life? I'm looking for reasons why."

Gladys found another reading. "This person was really interested in being psychic, but here is what Mr. Cayce advised: 'Pursue rather spiritual development; this is of the psychic nature, yes, but find the spirit first—not spiritualism, but spiritually in thy own life.'"[1]

Al sighed. "I thought that was what I *was* doing."

He recalled part of the first session, when he had been a monk, a priest of some sort, a man who was a professional in the religious field. That might have been a clue. Was there a connection with that windstorm and the crosses, the wrenching scene at the end of the first session?

The evening of June 5, after Dr. George had tried to sort out the facts from "James's" life and apparently concluded that this James didn't fit into the history background, he thought it was a good idea to search for more lives.

"Would you like to go further back?"

With eyes closed Al heaved a long sigh: "I'd *love* to."

Told to bring up what he remembered, to give his name, he took slow, deep breaths, then murmured, "1450. I was a monk. Italy . . . Name? . . . (barely audible) . . . I can't remember."

Men in religious orders were typically given other names than their own: Brother Sebastian, Brother John—but the doctor had asked for *his* name. Not the religious name.

"What part of Italy were you in?"

"Naples. But I didn't stay there long. I lived up in the . . . Something about columns at the top of a mountain near Naples." Not far from Naples, columns of old Greek and Roman temples, such as those at Metapont, reach to the sky. Snow-capped mountains are visible from some parts of the coast, as well.

A couple of the group hadn't thought of a mountain near Naples, only of grottoes. But the Apennine Mountains run like a backbone along Italy, on through even to Sicily, where Mt. Etna sometimes smokes the sky.

If this was Italy in the fifteenth century and if 1450 was the year beginning his life and activities as a monk, a quick look at the historical reference showed there would be much worth remembering, the greater part shadowed with horror.

Italy like the rest of Europe was recovering from the terrors of the Black Plague, the bubonic-pneumonic plague that had killed more men, women, and children than any war in history. The unspeakable Black Death had come to Italy from the Near East in 1348 and, close to a century later, the horror was finally receding. For the next hundred years the political and psychological effects would color the countryside. Parents would tell children who, in turn, would tell their children how it took barely three days to render most victims dark corpses, with bulbous lumps under the armpits, blood from the lungs frothy on the lips. It had cut the population of most lands by half or more.

This was a time for believing that God had tortured people for their sins, and groups of flagellants—whipping each other and loudly confessing their errors—had made their way throughout the land. Many then even blamed the priests and monks for shirking their duties. The priests, the monks, the friars (the word "friar" comes from the Latin *frater*, meaning "brother") had to set about placating an angry God and the citizens as well.

There were many: gray-robed friars, followers of Giovanni Francesco di Bernadone, later known as St. Francis; the followers of Domingo de Guzman, known as the Dominicans, sometimes called the Black Friars from the color of their robes; and the Carmelites, called White Friars, from their white robes. Even the Austin Friars (after St. Augustine), though we do not have the color of their robes.

So he had been a monk. The next question, of course:

"Do you remember the order?"

"I was . . . " (a whispered mumble) " 'ican."

It did not occur to the group that this might have been part of the word "Dominican," the "Black Friars."

"Did you wear a brown robe or a black robe or a gray robe?"

The answer came in a stern voice, as to someone who ought to know this:

"A black robe. A black robe!" he repeated.

Then Dr. George asked, "Were you a Jesuit?"

"*Yes* (firmly, with authority)."

A reference showed that 1534, some eighty years later, was the time of the first meeting of some followers with St. Ignatius of Loyola, a former soldier who believed this fellowship should practice poverty, chastity, and obedience; it later became the Society of Jesus, known as Jesuits. If 1450 was the friar's birth date, he would be "eighty-something" at this time. Was there a discrepancy in the dates? Or had he joined this group as an old-age activist, after a long career as a black-robed Dominican?

That would fit well with the other circumstances. The "Order of Friars Preachers," the original name of the order founded by de Guzman, filled a special need in the thirteenth and fourteenth century. These preachers living in poverty were to travel to various cities to minister to urban laity, as well as to combat heresies in northern Italy and southern France. In the years following 1450, they played a strong part in the beginnings of the Reformation—on both sides of the faith. The established faiths were supposed to cooperate with the activities of the group founded to quash all heresies: the Inquisition. Though the earliest of the succession of inquisitions was in 1050 A.D. and another wave some 300 years later, by the fifteenth century more fears were developing about witchcraft than about heresies, and the emphasis shifted to hunting witches and prosecuting sorcery. In this atmosphere, everyone—including friars and preachers—learned to be extremely careful of what they said.

Dr. George sought details.

"Where were you sent?"

"Rome."

"Were there many Jesuit priests at that time?"

"Twenty." He would be speaking of the earliest ones, before it was a full-blown society.

"Who was the pope at that time?"

"Leo." (Actually, Leo X was made pope in 1513.)

"Who was the king of Naples?"

No answer.

Considering that the top religious and political figures at this time were dealing in internecine struggles, and there were no newspapers or radio in those days to remind people of what was going on in the political field, this was not a time to discuss politics with a stranger. Kings and even popes could change with political winds, as happened when the Great Schism put in a second pope after thirteen cardinals objected to the first one, and the splitting effects echoed throughout Europe from 1378 to 1415. Clearly silence was the safest answer to a question like that, particularly if you were a friar.

The historical reference showed that Naples by this time was also known as the Kingdom of Two Sicilies and had long been dominated by the Medici family until invaded briefly by Charles VIII of France at the end of the fifteenth century. Finally it reverted to the control of Aragon, eastern Spain. This was followed by a spate of minor wars and re-alliances, but Spain stayed in control of the area up to a century after Columbus.

The doctor decided to check in another direction.

"What else did you do after you left Rome?"

"I didn't stay with other monks any more."

"Did you go and live by yourself?"

"Yes, I did live by myself. Far away from . . . "

But Henry George wanted additional connections.

"Did you know Savonarola in Florence?"

"No, I didn't meet him. I know that name." The friar answered the question with *both* meanings of the word "know"—he had not been acquainted with the man personally, but he recognized his name.

Interesting that Jerome Savonarola, who was a Dominican prior at the famous San Marco church in Florence, had the reputation of being a dictator and was known for zealous cruelty and for his burning of works of art. He was executed in 1498. Not strange that this friar knew his name.

"Did you know Galileo?"

Silence followed. It was hardly likely that anyone born in 1450 would even be alive at the time of Galileo (born in 1564, when the friar would be 114, an overripe age, at least)—let alone a later period when Galileo had become famous.

"Was Michelangelo there?"

"Michelangelo . . . painter. Is that who you mean? I watched him paint one time. Venice. Along the water. Painting a madonna. Brown . . . a halo, blackish hair, beautiful painting. Days he spent, weeks. I watched him paint it."

"Was it in a chapel?"

"No. He was painting it along the water."

Someone giving answers from current memory might have recalled the Sistine Chapel and said yes, but this friar said no. He recalled only watching the artist by the water. And while there are many such places near Venice, it's also possible that the place was Florence. Without a suggested date as to when he might have seen Michelangelo, we might wonder if this was the period when the artist as a young teen was apprenticed to the painter Ghirlandajo, around

1487. Later, the artist made it clear that he preferred sculpture, even though he was practically compelled by Pope Julius II to paint the Sistine Chapel. By this time, he was quite well known to the major families—including the Medici enclave—in Italy, and unless the friar was really staying away from people, he would answer the next question differently:

"Was Michelangelo appreciated?"

"No. Not when I knew him, he wasn't." Later he added, "I didn't know or understand about painting, but I just used to watch him. I didn't understand him."

"How old a man was he?"

"Thirty, that I know of. I lost sight of him."

So far, these answers have been polite, straightforward, anything but verbose—as might well be expected from someone accustomed to long periods of solitary meditation. Nothing like Jack, nothing like the frightened Pierre, nor the gentle James.

Now, the doctor wanted to investigate the details of this religious life.

"Can you give us some of the ritual that you used in your order?"

"It isn't allowed to give."

This is a word-for-word translation of the Latin expression, *Non licet dare.* "It is not permitted to give." The ritual would be in Latin. There was a strong feeling against revealing it to the uninitiated.

"Who was the commander of your order?"

Silence.

This man was in control of his tongue, much more so than Jack or young James.

"Could you sing us some of the hymns? Would you sing us one of the hymns that your order sang?"

Silence.

To the hypnotized man, the questioner was obviously not

one of his order. But he would not be rude to the questioner. He simply stayed quiet.

"You do not care to answer. Would you tell us how you greeted your friends? What salutation did you use? You will bring this up in your memory. You will recall how you greeted your friends, and you will greet me as you greeted your friends."

This time, the silence was broken. "Sah-weh." (*Salve*, in classical Latin pronounced sahl-weh, is the Roman greeting "Hail.")

"Did you speak Italian at that time? Could you describe for us the weather?"

"Where?" A sensible response to the last question. Italy's varied topography could have different weather patterns on the coast, in the valleys, and on the mountains.

"In the mountains when you retired alone."

"There was snow, snow all the time. Fifty miles from Naples, and I was in a cave up there. It was deep . . . among the trees."

"Did you pray a lot?"

"All the time."

"To yourself or out loud?"

"Both. Mostly out loud."

This was customary, prayers aloud to God so any listeners would know you were doing your religious duty in these painful times, just as the flagellants cried out their distress and sorrow so their countrymen would know the whippings were making them repent.

"Would you repeat some of your prayers for us?"

Hesitation, then "—Laude, laude Patrem . . . "

Al's voice began to trail off. Fitting indeed after he had just spoken the Latin words, "Praise, praise to the Father."

If these words held the power of prayer, even the prayer of a hypnotized man, you would expect something unusual to happen.

Henry George and the witnesses waited.

"I feel," the voice sounded far off, "like I'm in-between somewhere and somewhere else."

Dr. George offered soothing words, then asked, "You have traveled far, would you like to travel further?"

"It's a big jump. I can't make it," the voice said faintly. Then he did make it. And he arrived in a lifetime with incredible memories. But the life he leaped to began in 5 B.C. This life was visited in every session. We have collected the happenings from that life into chapter 9.

There is also a value in seeing the chronological changes, the sequential events, the emotional links and connections in reverse order. It will be helpful to see where he was just before he came to this austere, ascetic life as a black-robed friar, first a Dominican and then a Jesuit.

7

Sun, Sand, and Song

Time travel had been easier during the second session. Sinking through the clouds of the past on June 5, Al had gone from his life—and his death—as Jack Carstairs, down past little Pierre, past the attempts to be helpful as British James, on to the austere Italian priest who, this time, had mentioned almost enviously watching an artist at work.

Dr. George wondered now whether he should try to steer his volunteer to a life near to that of the friar. In the first session, after the friar had uttered the Latin prayer, he had seemingly hung in-between ages, in-between existences, until he had landed in a life that was almost 1,500 years in the past. This time, the doctor had noted the friar beginning a child-like reaction to questions, similar to the child-like reaction toward the end of questioning James, and he suspected fatigue might be a problem. They had not even begun the session until after 9:30 p.m.

After his subject commented about the artist he watched, "They sure could paint, though, that fellow Angelo sure could paint," Dr. George interrupted.

"Will you go back further for us." Maybe he would find a place only 100 or so years earlier, before the subject got too tired to give clear answers.

Al sighed, three slow sighs. "Ummm . . . " He seemed at ease.

"Tell us what you see."

"Nine hundred fifty-two," the observer gave the year; the place, "Tripoli. I was colored. Heat. Many sands." ("Colored" was the term commonly used in 1952 when white people spoke about black people or African-Americans.)

The questioner wanted to be sure. "What was your race?"

The observer clarified it: "Tripoli—Tripolitan, black race. I lived in Tripoli." Then he described the surroundings. "There is sand all over the place. All of it is sand." (Tripoli is in North Africa, part of Libya, on the Mediterranean seacoast.)

The listeners wondered how the doctor would handle this news. This was a far contrast from the place where the priest spent most of his time, in a cave on a snow-capped mountain. The hot sands of Tripoli, no less. And a black, not a white man.

Dr. George recalled that, as Jack Carstairs, he had a wife and a girl friend; as "James," he had a girl friend. This time? He asked, "Were you married?"

"No—no interest." That sounded more like the priest than like Jack or James.

The doctor decided to ask, "Were you ever a woman?" He believed the subject could see easily into other lifetimes, and he had already had several cases in his files of people who had past lives in both genders.

His subject replied simply, "Never was." He added, in an agreeable manner, "Not that I can remember. Maybe I can't remember back far enough."

There was something different about this person.

Suddenly the man on the couch burst into resonant syllables, in a powerful, deep voice: "Yong, bong, jong, ing, yong bong jong!"

The startled witnesses sat upright. The doctor asked, "What does that mean?"

"Wheeng yung dung wheeng!" the strong vocals continued. Then the Tripolitan explained, "Lot of people all over. We're all having a time. Yeah. Drums." He seemed to be listening to them. "We don't do any work, just sing. The sun is out . . . Sand . . . there is sand all over the place." This man was not rattling off geography and statistics; he was just expressing happiness.

It seemed almost the opposite of the life of the simple priest. Warmth and comfort, all from nature. None of that snow the priest found in the mountains, just sun and sand and music.

Since he had just regressed Al from the life of a friar, who was probably a Jesuit, and Al had been so interested in the spiritual, Dr. George asked, "What religion were you?"

"Don't have any. I'm not interested in any of that. A lot of bunk and superstition."

This was a shocking contrast to the priest's life—and to all the others he had experienced so far. The Hebrew watching the crucifixion had been visibly moved. "James" was proper Church of England. Little Pierre "saw" Jesus. Jack Carstairs had been trying to understand. But this black man called it "bunk and superstition"! What could have made this life so different?

"Are you a slave?"

"No, I'm not a slave. We just have a good time."

Was this a classical idyllic life on the North African coast? One of the witnesses remembered the story of Odysseus wandering the Mediterranean and coming to "The Land of the Lotus-Eaters," people who wanted nothing but pleasure.

"Were there any musicians?" Dr. George would explore what he could.

"Oh, yeah."

"What kind of instruments did they play?"

"Zithers and harps . . . and a lot of others. A drum made of camel skin." (The drum *head* is usually of skin.)

Did they have any weapons? Yes, bows and arrows. And stones. Maybe this tribe's men were warlike savages after all. But the smiling man assured them, "I didn't fight, I don't bother to fight when we can sing!" Indeed, the unspoken thought of a listener: If only the rest of the world were like that!

"Were you a singer?"

"No, no! We *all* sing, all of us." The man seemed to think "a singer" meant "a soloist." He seemed fearful of being considered a "loner," of doing something all by himself. Evidently his life was so filled with friends, he would not want to step ahead of anyone else. No desire to perform; he wanted only to be with the group.

"Will you sing a song for us?" There was a pause. "Do you remember a song?"

"Too hot. Too hot now to sing. We only sing in the cool nighttime." This was June 5, 1952, not a hot night. The temperature Al felt was from that lifetime, not the present.

Dr. George coaxed: "What did you sing in the cool nighttime?"

"It's too hot now. We sang all kinds of songs . . . You wouldn't like it."

Dr. George was not deterred; he continued to urge, the singer continued to demur and make excuses. "Our songs—well, like it's awful loud. We made an awful lot of noise."

"We like those songs."

Still no singing. Well, if he would not sing, they could learn something else. "How did you address your friends?"

"'Sahaidid, sahaidid, sahaidid,' was for our friends. 'Sahaidid.'"

Maybe if they asked for just one? "Please sing one song," said the doctor, "as loud as you like."

The black Tripolitan protested again, was encouraged again, then said a lot of them would have to sing. Perhaps if he changed the kind of question: "Will you give us the meaning of your song?"

"Which one?

"Your favorite."

"'Pretty sky, pretty sun, laughing girls, laughing sun, *Sing, all life—all life's a song.*' " Suddenly he broke into unknown syllables and sang with wholehearted abandon. The doctor and witnesses were entranced.

"That is beautiful. Will you sing it again?"

There seemed to be a sharp difference in the perception of sound. The Tripolitan expected the feeling of singing in the open air but the reverberations within the confines of the room's four walls were different. He protested, "That was too loud. We had all space, and in all space it didn't sound that loud, but sounded soft." His voice was fading. "We had all space." He knew he wasn't out on the sand now. "I feel very tired . . . very tired."

"Well, you rest," the soothing voice agreed, "You rest."

Here was the black man's first appearance. The fifth life they had located for Al. A cautious, gentle, happy, modest man, but one who could express volumes—literally—when he sang those joyous songs with friends. Nothing solo here. A far cry from the other lives.

Because this was the first time in Al's past-life experiences that the theme, "All life's a song," had come up, along with joy and gladness and living with nature, the hypnotist knew this would be a safe life to revisit, a life he could lead the subject to if he were upset or troubled in another period. It would be like a refresher for times when he was not feeling well. Henry George felt sure he would return to it again and again.

Since his subject had apparently gathered more energy during this life on the Mediterranean coast, the doctor thought he might use the energy to go back to the life as a Jew to gather more information. He did. Achmesh told of Roman soldiers bullying the Jews and gave other details of the experience, enough to give Dr. George the idea of having a linguist who could speak Hebrew for a future session.

There was something different about that black man. He hadn't given his name. He had tried hard to avoid anything that looked like showing off. He held no fear, no worries, no animosity. It could be healing just to remember that life.

In the third session, just a week later on June 12, when the doctor had taken his subject back through Jack Carstairs's life, they came to a place where the hypnotized man kept repeating, "I shouldn't have done that, shouldn't have done that"—then Henry George wanted to make him feel happy again. He knew the life that would do it.

"I want you to go back to 952, when you were in Tripoli; you were very happy there."

Al first protested, "It's a long ways." Then he was asked, "Do you wish to go?" The instant reply was, "Oh, I want to go there!"

It was not to be rushed. "Give me time," he murmured, then after a pause, "Wait a minute. Nine hundred fifty-two . . . yeah, yeah.

"Oh, look at all them stars, oh, they're beautiful, oh! That's grandeur!" ("Them stars" was not Al's usual language, but neither was ecstasy his usual expression!)

This life held euphoria, with exhilaration over the beauty of the sun and stars! None of the other lives had shown that. A life with no guilt, no intrigue, no cheating, no enemies—just songs and friends. And what else?

"There are forty of us now. Let's see." The observer is locating and describing the surroundings. "It's somewhere . . . I see the Mediterranean—or is it the ocean? No, the Mediterranean. About four miles from the Mediterranean Ocean . . . wait a minute, sort of rolling sand, dunes. We had white pajamas on, all of us. We are all of us shaved, we're all . . . dirty, sand and all, had white robes but they were dirty, too." He didn't seem to mind the dirt and sand, which had bothered him greatly when he was a Jew. "They (the robes) come over our heads, you know, to protect from the sun, but this is nighttime."

"And it is at night that you . . . "

Al interrupted. "It's night. Oh, we sing! That's all we ever do! It's wonderful. Just sing. Nobody works, what's the sense of working?"

Smiling to themselves, the witnesses nodded, although one later confessed he wondered if this was pure laziness. They were to learn that answer later. Dr. George said they would be happy to have this man sing.

The Tripolitan sidestepped the suggestion, saying instead, like a host introducing guests to his estate, "There's an oasis, and you go get a drink of water if you want any. I'll tell you the name of the town in a minute, where it's a whole lot of little huts, a little ways away. Palm trees growing near the huts, a whole lot, must be fifty of them. We're just sitting around all together and . . . we feel cool, because the Mediterranean Ocean has breezes that drift in from the north. Some fellow, one of the boys, has a harp, and he's playing. Isn't 'at purty?" His accent was changing, very relaxed.

Dr. George again coaxed him to sing, but again Al resisted, urging him to listen to *everyone*.

How could the hypnotist explain to the entranced man that only *Al* could hear the other singers? He changed the emphasis: "We'd like to hear *you* sing."

Still reluctant. "Let me listen to them awhile and maybe I can get the tune."

They waited patiently, then the Tripolitan warned, "You'll be startled out of your wits, you'd better not!"

The doctor protested that they did like his songs. "Please sing them for us."

"The one they are singing is 'Drun Dung.' " Apparently joining in with the unseen singers, he offered a loud, rhythmic song.

"Beautiful," said the doctor.

"I wish I could sing like the other fellows do."

"You sing beautifully." This singer was too modest.

"It's so pretty. The stars—it seems like you could just jump all over the stars, and the boys all are singing, such pretty voices. And we sleep right out in the sand . . . " his voice sounded more distant.

"Please sing us another song before you leave the campfire."

Dr. George had picked up the wrong image.

"Fire? We didn't have fire. Tonight it was warm, the breezes weren't cold enough. We don't have any fire tonight, it's so nice." He didn't seem to hear the doctor's request for another song; he was listening to something.

"They're still singing the same song. Wait a minute, they're going to start another one. Now wait . . . " and he described the leader of their group.

"Longo, he's a big black man, he's got gold beads around a . . . (word not understood) with his hair knotted up. He's going to start the next song—'Aliman, Aliman,' that's the name of it." The subject listened for a moment, then let his powerful voice go: "Nocha, Nocha, Aliman, Nocha, Nocha, Aliman, Nocha, Nocha, Aliman, Aliman . . . " When he stopped, he gave a happy cry, "Hey, Longo, that's pretty!"

The witnesses half expected Longo to reply.

"Will you tell us what it means?"

"Aliman means twilight stars. It means . . . about the world, 'The stars will always gleam in the hearts of men.' That's my native language. I'm of the tribe—Longo is our leader—of the tribe of Nocha."

The singer was to offer similar poetic imagery, often translating feelings as much as words, from this lifetime.

But Dr. George had data to gather. "Where do you people come from originally?"

"You mean where was I born?"

"And where did your father and your father's father come from?" This man's vocabulary was not that of the other lives. Unlike the others, he hadn't given his name, only the name of their beloved leader. What would make a man feel so attached to a leader?

"Egypt, we came from Egypt, he (father) came from Egypt, a long line of descendants. We were slaves; we got away, we got to Tripoli. All we do is sing. We don't want to fight." He emphasized it again, "We don't want to fight, we don't want to be slaves, just sing." He broke into the rhythmic chant, "Aliman, Aliman, Nocha, Nocha! We just sing, sing all those things that go back to Egypt, the beatings, the whippings."

Then, as the witnesses and the doctor listened, for the first time he told of his childhood, where he was one of several black slave families under the Egyptian rulers. His father was one of the royal slaves. Worse, he was a boat slave, one of those whose skill would steer the princess in her royal barge along the Nile. His father was rowing one day and the lad heard the princess scream at him. "I remember," he told the doctor, "when I was a little boy, my father got whipped, with red welts on his back 'cause he wouldn't row some princess down the Nile, wouldn't row hard enough, and she beat him." His father was beaten so badly, his back so raw, that he couldn't row. And slaves who couldn't do their work—well . . . "I said, 'Oh, boy, I've got to escape.' "

There was a concerted movement of the black slaves and somehow, "We all got out of Egypt—we ran away." And now, "We just sing," he added, "sing all those things that go back to Egypt." So beneath all this light-hearted happiness was the heartbreak of the children, remembering why they had to run away and how.

Perhaps providentially, this was about the time a group of Muslims called the "Fatimids"—claiming descent from Fatima, the daughter of Mohammed—gained control over much of north Africa, starting in the year 909. These conquerors continued their spread, founding a new capital, Cairo, in Egypt in 969. It could have been far easier for slaves to escape when invaders were taking over the country.

The black man continued, "Then these people adopted me on the desert. I didn't want to have anything to do with any women after that princess beat my father. Nothing but pain. We were just happy, we wanted to sing."

He broke into song again: "Aliman, Aliman, Nocha, Nocha. Oh, night, it's so wonderful!" As if getting warmed up, he burst out again, "Aliman, Nocha, Nocha, Aliman, Nocha, Nocha!" Then, quietly, "We just sing."

Dr. George asked, "Are there any women in this tribe?"

"No, no use for women. We're happy."

"Why are there no women in this tribe?"

"We don't want them." He repeated the story of the Egyptian princess. "We don't want any women in this land. All they want is jewels and persecuting men. We're happy, in Longo's tribe, we're happy."

"And what do you do?"

"Sing, that's all, sing. Go to sleep and sing, wake up and sing, go to sleep, sing." They were covering their grief with music, pretending it wasn't there.

But surely, the doctor knew, they had to have something to eat. "What is your food?"

"Well," said the former slave with humorous appreciation, "some of the people in these huts are crazy enough to work and they like us and they like our singing, so when we're hungry we come in town, and they give us gourds of water, and there's a kind of baked palm leaves we eat. It wasn't bad; we ate alligator pears. We didn't call it that, though. And fruits, and anything we find. We used to go down to the seashore and catch fish with our hands, grab 'em right out of the water.[1] Oh, they were good! We catch 'em, cook 'em right on the fire. Palm trees, leaves blowin' in the breeze, everything lovely . . . "

Only one conclusion possible, Dr. George agreed. "You were very happy and your people were very happy."

Now the doctor wanted some more details besides food. "What did you make your clothing out of?"

"Trees . . . There was a tree, besides the palm tree, we called it . . . I don't think I can say it in English . . . 'Escalpiers' tree, and that is what we made clothing out of." (*Eucalyptus* is the name of a tree of the Myrtales family which also grows well in Africa. In warmer areas, the *Encyclopaedia Britannica* says, they are often woody shrubs, and the *paperbark* tree is one of its relatives. Its Latin name is *Melaleuca leucadendron.* This does NOT sound like "Escalpier," however.) "It was very easy, you just beat it, it's sort of bark, you unwound," the subject had said. In the *Encyclopedia of Textiles* by Judith Jerde, bark cloth is made by beating the inner bark of certain trees and shrubs into a fibrous, "felted" fabric. They beat and soak the wood, including the "breadfruit tree" or "paper mulberry"—it is still created in Vietnam and some South Pacific islands and, according to the *Britannica,* has a variety native to tropical Africa, *Treculia africana.* (In the South Seas, cloth is made from the fibrous inner bark, wood of the tree is used for canoes and furniture, and glue and caulking material are obtained from the milky juice.) But 1,400 years ago it may well have been widely spread. The encyclopedia says it is usually painted when used as clothing. Rayon, of course, is made from wood, treated with chemicals. Hemp, however, comes from a plant more like a shrub than a tree. The bark of some trees comes off in shreds, almost ready for weaving.[2]

They had all they needed: friends, food, clothing. "You were happy," the hypnotist prompted.

"All happiness!" the singer agreed. "All my life I'm happy. All the people, all of us are happy."

"Did you have a family?"

"No, then I wouldn't be happy." Did he have some foreknowledge that every time he started to have a family in future lives, there would be heartache? "I didn't have anything, just me," he explained simply. "Most of us, under Longo, just used to eat and sing, and could we sing! And then we'd go in and swim and then we'd sing 'cause we're happy when we come out again. Catch fish and go in swimming again. Eat, lie down, go to sleep and sing."

He went into another chorus of "Aliman, Aliman, Nocha, Nocha, Aliman," adding, "u drum i drum di ungi dong, Aliman."

The doctor wanted more, but the answer surprised him: "Longo says it's time to go to sleep, it's late."

"That was very happy," said the doctor gently.

The smiling sleeper murmured, "Very happy, very happy."

"You will remember those happy memories, too."

"Always. Sometimes I remember hundreds of songs we sing. I have to go, Longo says. But some time sing, there's hundreds of 'em. Everything was happiness." "Longo," in this lifetime in the 900s, was also a protective being, almost a guardian.

Henry George noticed this was the first life experience in which someone within Al's past life was telling him it was time to go. He acceded. But he knew they would have to bring back the black singer *and* Longo.

In fact, it was during the fourth session, held at Virginia Beach—the one specially arranged because of Gladys Davis's concern so that she would feel reassured about her fiancé's continuing trance experiences—that Dr. George brought forth the Tripolitan life again. (The others, too, for research, of course.)

He looked forward to that unusual combination of emotions that came from the singer: joy, humility, reluctance, ecstasy, and the unique full-throated song.

Not at night, but at 11 o'clock in the morning, this was the only one of the eight sessions to be held in the daytime.

Dr. George might be excused for feeling a bit tense with these witnesses, including Edgar Cayce's son and Al's fiancée, going through Al's hidden lives. Skillfully he led Al, in trance, through several lives, then quickly to the happy time in North Africa.

"In Tripoli—there you were under the leadership of Longo. Will you describe Longo for us?" He somehow expected Al to make an immediate transition.

But the man in trance murmured, "It's very dark. It's a long way."

Henry George realized he could not rush this. "You have the power, and take the time. You go back."

"It's a long way. (A heavy sigh.) Yeah, yeah." (The excitement was beginning to return, but he spoke as if the observer was directing him, like a teacher ordering a pupil to recite. This was not the spontaneous speech of the last meeting with Longo's friend, more like that of a first-grader, reciting. Or an unemotional observer, giving simple facts.) "I see him. Longo is tall, six feet six inches. Tall, bushy hair, black hair, very black. The year, 954 A.D. The country is Tripoli. My race is colored. We are all dark skinned. We are very happy. Longo is the greatest of all our tribe. In English the tribe would be called Mushma. (Could he have meant Muslim?) Longo is the leader. Nothing but happiness exists in this country. All is happiness. The creator has given his power to this tribe to make men happy. Longo is greatest. He plays the zither and we all sing. Always sing."

If Dr. George wondered about the personality using these short juvenile sentences instead of his previous lyric speech, he didn't show it.

This time he did not ask, he ordered: "Now you will sing for us. Now you will sing."

"There are so many songs. Which one?"

"Will you sing for us your 'Aliman' song? We like that song."

But Al gave the translation, not the original words: "Blue sky, blue heavens, cast a glow." Then he shifted. "Longo, tonight is cold. (Set) the fireplace, and we'll sing. (We'll put) the sticks in the sand. There are so many there; tonight there are over a thousand people. All of us are colored race and we are happy."

Dr. George reminded him, "And you will sing for us."

Now it happens. In full voice, Al bursts out, " 'Aliman, Aliman, Aliman, Longo, Longo, Aliman, Aliman oogi ul!' We sing much louder, much louder, but it's too loud."

"We like those songs," Henry George encouraged him. "You will listen to them sing another song and then you will sing that for us."

"There's one, 'Do le, so le, do le, do le, Aliman, Aliman, uigi, uigi . . . ' " (He continues for several minutes.)

"That was lovely. And will you sing for us your Aliman Nocha Nocha?"

This time, with rhythmic fervor, the singer gave the original words, "Nocha, Nocha, Aliman, Nocha, Nocha, Aliman, Nocha, Nocha, Aliman, Aliman, Aliman." The beat was strong and joyous. "You know what that means in English?"

"You tell us what that means."

"As the stars glow, the lovely fragrance of the dunes cast forth brilliance upon the Mediterranean, as Longo and the tribe rest." The personality had returned to the lyrical one. The words appeared to symbolize a poet's appreciation of the surrounding sea, sand, and stars and could be rendered by any English words that gave the feeling.

"Are there any women in this tribe?"

"No, no use for women. We're happy in Longo's tribe."

"What do you eat?"

"The leaves of the trees, mangoes, fish. It's right on the Mediterranean Ocean, and there are plenty of fish. You just walk in and pick them up. Net them. Pick them up. Plenty to eat."

"What kind of weapons do you use?"

"Stones, stone hammers. Bows and arrows."

"Do you have any enemies?"

"None. We don't believe in enemies. Just singing and go to sleep and some more sing." This was the happy primitive. If only they all could live that way. The listeners looked at each other and smiled.

Dr. George asked him to sing again, and he did, then he added, "We love our Longo. He always stands in the middle. We're always in a circle."

"He is just with you?"

"He is there now. I wish I could sing like him. He has a voice of the angels." The more he speaks of Longo, the more eloquent he becomes.

"Will you sing again for us?"

Al did and was asked to explain the song. "Nocha Nocha means 'God be praised. In His infinite wisdom, He has given us life.' That's all."

"Your people are deeply religious," Dr. George commented, recalling the earlier period when the black man said he had no time for that sort of junk.

"I believe in God." This was not an acceptance of religious ritual, it appeared, but a belief in a power, a personal "something" to worship. Asked if he had any symbols of God, he answered simply, "The stars."

Trying to pin him down, the doctor asked, "Do you have any *man-made* symbols of God?"

"No. The stars. I think He's up in the stars there, watching and making us happy."

"Do your people also worship the sun and the moon?"

"That's right. The sun makes the sand hot and makes the day hot. The sun is to be worshiped."

"And the moon?"

"The moon makes us cool nights. The mother of the earth, and . . . helps the tides."

Carefully continuing, Dr. George asked him to say a few words "of your tongue."

The courteous response: "What would you want to hear?"

"Will you come and drink water with me?"

He spoke, but since we have no machine recording of this session and this typist did not transliterate or try to spell out the strange words, we know only that he did talk.

"And we say, 'We will part in peace.' Won't you say that?"

"Shalom." This appears to be the observer answering, for the observer could bring a word like "Shalom" from the Hebrew life or even from current knowledge.

The doctor returned, "Shalom," and instructed, "Now you will rest with Longo and his friends. You are very happy. And will you bring out the happiest recollection of this life with Longo and tell us about it? The high point?"

There was a pause, then, "Longo got married."

With evident satisfaction, Dr. George exclaimed, "Then there was a woman!" The witnesses could feel a silent "Aha!"

"That's it."

"Only one woman in the tribe?" Hard to believe.

"No." The subject explained: "She wasn't *in* the tribe. She *came*. Longo rescued her, at an oasis, and brought her to the tribe and brought her back to health and fell in agonies (he must have meant 'in love') with her and he married. We didn't want to lose Longo, and we wanted to see him happy, because he made us happy, so I guess that was the happiest, when Longo got married." Love for Longo overcame the tribe's disgust with women.

"And did you sing to him?"

"We all sang, all the time sang." (Here again this is not the usual English order of words.)

"What did you sing to him when he got married?"

"A wedding song."

"Will you sing the wedding song?"

The singer had to explain: "We made that for Longo. All of us were happy. It was cold that night. J-x-w-i was the girl's name. Longo dressed her up in leaves of the unga tree." (This reminded one witness of the Hawaiians dressed in grass skirts.)

In a moment the black man sang emotional poetic syllables, an apparent acceptance of Longo's love for a woman as well as his men, and their love for Longo—"We wanted to see him happy because he made us happy"—and this feeling turned into a rendition of the song.

Reassuring, Dr. George said softly, "He was very happy with that, I'm sure."

But before he brought Al from this life, he wanted to know, "Will you tell us how you met your death when you were with Longo?"

The observer's answer was brief. "Twenty-seven years old; 956 A.D. Swimming, not too far out. Fish, big fish, I guess shark, bit off leg right below the knee cap." He was silent.

"You need not dwell on that," said the doctor.

LONGO: PLAYER, POET, TEACHER

Toward the end of the sixth session, on July 10, Al had come through a peak emotional experience of his life as Achmesh, and Dr. George wanted him to experience some relaxation and happiness before returning to the present.

"And as you come back across the years, will you stop with Longo, in Tripoli?"

Slowly the subject's face relaxed, then gradually he began laughing. "That's the funniest thing I ever saw. Some guy is dancing, he's got a blue cap. He's dancing on his hands!—with a yellow necklace."

First time *this* happened. "What year is this?"

"Nine hundred fifty-six A.D."

"Is Longo there?"

"Yes. He never leaves us. He and they sing."

By now Dr. George knew how to bring the music: "Will you catch a tune for us and sing it?"

"Yes, that's all they ever do, sing and fish, eat and swim and sing. Us colored people know how to live." Relaxed, smiling, he bursts into full-throated song.

"That was a fine song. What does it mean?"

" 'We take of God's will and make it into joy. The joy we have is today, today is ours.' That's all." Then he explained, "It's in the language of Nubran (sounded on the tape like Nubian), that is the name of the language we used."

He signaled that he was tired and received permission: "You will rest and come back over the years."

Meeting on the warm evening, July 15, 1952, in the Drexelbrook home of one of the Theosophists, Dr. George again brought the life with Longo back to comfort his subject, who had just gone through the experience of freezing to death in Siberia.

Thoughtfully, the doctor led him to the life in the sand and the sun of Tripoli. "And now will you tell us more about Longo? and sing us one of his songs?"

"He's asleep now. I'll have to wake him up. We'd eaten a lot of fish. An' it's good, too."

"Does he mind being awakened?"

"No, Longo doesn't mind anything. He's sweet to everybody. Never cross, never angry. Always helps everybody. He says I can sing the *one* song, but he wishes *he* could sing it for you *right*, 'cause it's a difficult song. He doesn't think I'm good enough."

"Well, *he* may not think you're good enough, but *we* think you are. Won't you please sing it for us?"

"I'll have to ask him. Hmmm, I'll try. It's hard to sing. Longo's so beautiful. His is so much better . . . but I'll try."

At top volume, he roars:

"Buch-la, runna runna, Buch-la, runna runna, Bungla rungla gungla gunga, Nucca nucca, Buuchla Buch-la, rundo, rundo, rundo, rundo, (softly) nucca, nucca, gungla gungla, gong bong jong gong gong!"

Dr. George made the only fit comment: "Well, that was certainly interesting!"

There was no acceptance of praise, just a long sigh. "It's hard." Asked to tell what it meant, the sleeper explained, "Longo taught us to sing to get rhythm. The song meant:

" 'Move around. Stand up straight. Move around. Keep your feet constantly in motion, always making sure not to kick anyone with your bare feet, or he will kick you. And don't kick sand in anybody's face.' "

The witnesses tried to keep straight faces.

Dr. George had more information both he and Al wanted to know about Longo. This would be a time to ask:

" . . . And had you known Longo before? He was a great man, a kind, a just man. Who was Longo?"

Speaking as the observer, Al related, "In a previous experience, Longo was St. Paul. Longo now is John Foster Dulles. Longo has all knowledge, he knew where the stars came from; he tries to teach us. (In) 950. He used to spend day after day teaching us all. The twenty of us as we sat there in a circle." As one who adored Longo, Al spoke:

"He taught us to sing, to love God,
who was the Stars and the Moon.
He told us why the stars were up there,
to make us better and stronger.
He taught us that the moon was our mother.
He divided up our wage each night.
He told us that the sun made the earth retain the heat

So that we would be warm at night after the sun left.
He taught us everything.
He was all-wise Father, Longo was.
Most of all, he taught us to sing.

8

Cold Night of the Soul

July 15, 1952.

On this hot and humid evening, the witnesses sat quietly in the suburban Philadelphia living room watching Dr. George put his subject in a trance. Then the doctor directed Al to go back in time, to look for the scene of the stoning of Stephen.

As Al began speaking, it was clear he was not around Stephen. "There is an earthquake and a lot of shifting. An area over a hundred miles wide. No water . . . I'm on the planet Mars."

"You will go back," the doctor said. It would not help his research into the possibility of proving past lives to have anything show up about Mars. He hoped everyone would forget about this little aberration. He repeated firmly, "You will go back."

"I'm going back . . . " and the subject was again Achmesh, calling to Stephen. They passed through the painful scene of Stephen's stoning, and on . . .

Suspecting there were more earthly lives between Achmesh and the happy life in Tripoli, Henry George gave the specific suggestion, "And now I would like to have you, if you will, leave the experience of Achmesh and search out and find where next your individuality incarnated, and tell us about it." Going forward in time, Al found life as a Roman in the year 201. After learning of the Roman's life, Dr. George took his volunteer forward yet again. Since the order of his lives, as told in these pages, has been going from the present back in time, we will look at the story as it reached the nearest plateau to the 900s.

"And I would like to have you search for us and pick up again your experience upon this earth, as an individuality, telling us where you lived and who you were?"

As the circulating fan hummed in the warm night air, the man on the couch began to tense and tremble.

"It's cold. It's bitter cold." He seemed to be holding himself, trying not to shiver. Once again the observer self was able to say when this was occurring in the past millennia: "820 A.D."

"This was your next incarnation?" Dr. George asked.

"No," with a trace of impatience. "It's the one I'm in *now.* Siberia. It's fifty below zero."

"Will you tell us how old you are at this time? . . . and your name?"

"Forty-two . . . Peter." (He later added "Gregor.")

"What language do you speak?"

"I have a language you would not know."

"Will you greet us in it?"

"Oogra, Oogra . . . " the typist wrote.

"Ugric," a name which turned up in a search of information on Siberia, is one of the older ethnic groups in that sprawling, mysterious land. "Finno-Ugric" is one of the languages spoken. It is doubtful that either the doctor or witnesses *or* the subject were aware of that.

Asked what "Oogra" meant, he said, "Hello."

Anxious for more information, the doctor continued, "And will you say to us in your native tongue, 'Come and break bread with me'?"

"Oogra don oloi onsi doublet" (as the typist heard the sounds). The subject explained again, to the foreign questioner, "A language which you do not know. It is called the Semin, used by those tribes of Eskimos in northernmost Siberia in 820 A.D." (The Semitic language would sound close to this word; that is actually a term for two groups of languages. "Semin" as such is not listed but "Seman"—which might have been the sound actually spoken—is the root of the Greek word *semanein,* to show, to have meaning—hence, "semantic." What could be a fitter term for a language?)

Bringing up the type of spoken language in a country none of the participants or witnesses had visited was a sensible attempt to find some familiar link that could be investigated, but apparently Peter/Gregor was right. This portion of northeastern Siberia, which he said was several hundred miles northeast of Vladivostok, was practically Eskimo territory. There were a large number of very small ethnic groups in the area. And, according to the *Britannica,* this part of Siberia was mainly tundra, where some tribes kept fairly large herds of domestic reindeer, which became their principal means of nourishment. Gregor, however, might have been with one of the even more primitive nomadic groups which hunted wild reindeer and fished.

Frustrated that there seemed to be no apparent connection between that language and any of the languages this intellectual group was acquainted with, the doctor decided to find out how his subject got into his icy predicament.

"And what are you doing there? Are you a—"

"Freezing," was the painful, impatient answer. "Yes, I'm freezing. Freezing to death. I can't move."

"And why are you freezing to death there?" A reasonable question, since the temperature everyone else in the room felt was quite comfortable while the fan was blowing.

"I'm lost. I'm lost from my tribe," he said plaintively. "I fell into a glacial deposit. It's cold, awful cold."

It appears that this man was a hunter, who had gone out along the glacier seeking more wild reindeer and had fallen into the rift in the ice. Not difficult to envision, if the hunter was making his way on foot, without a dog sled, and in a snowstorm.

The only way for this conversation to continue was to go further back to a safer period. Henry George knew what to say: "Can you go back a few years in your life to when you were a young man?"

A moment of silence, as the breathing became more relaxed: "807 A.D. A town. Ograda." The companion observer continues: "475 miles north by east of what is now known as Vladivostock.[1] In this town the temperature never goes above zero. We live below ground. Our homes are deep underground, 100 feet down. It's the only way we can keep warm."

Although many dwellings in northern Siberia today, in the Eskimo areas, are portable, such as tents of skins in the summer, Gregor describes his tribe's homes as permanent, in caves, underground, reached by steps. Mountains stretch up and down this area, mountains formed by the earth's crinkling crust, which would make for variations in the land areas, similar to areas along the western coast of the Americas from the Aleutians down. Formation of underground caves in such places is sometimes a part of the process.

Now more about his daily life. "What do you wear?"

"We wear fur, fur of the arctic munst. It's a large animal—looks like a leopard. It is of the cat family and has lots of fur."

Though neither Dr. George nor any of the witnesses had heard of such an animal, this is an accurate description of the Siberian snow leopard, a beautiful animal but quite rare today. It is interesting to note that the snow leopard is also called the OUNCE—or UNCE—as in part of the word muUNSt.[2]

A garment of the snow leopard fur would indeed be the finest—as much of a luxury or status symbol, perhaps, as a coat of ranch mink or sable today. Later, Gregor admitted he also wore clothing of rabbit skins. Such animals were killed by the standard weapons, bow and arrow, and barbed spear with a head of mammoth or walrus ivory. How did they cook and keep warm? Of course, they had to have fire to survive in that northern land, and this was not difficult since they knew how. The tribes made fire in a way similar to that of the Native Americans: a shaft of hard wood was spun in a socket of stone, with a bowstring tightly circled about it so that when the short bow was drawn back and forth, the shaft would spin at high speed in the socket, where wood chips lay. The resulting heat would make the wood chips glow; and soon, fire.

Asked how the people lived, whether they lived in families or clans, Al answered, "We live in tribes. There are 120 of us, and underground we have each a little room, coming up by stone stairs." (Similar to some of the cave areas of the Southwest, as well as to those caves described in Jean Auel's *Clan of the Cave Bear* which led far within a mountainside.)

"And what food do you eat? And are you married?"

As he often did when asked two questions at one time, he answered the last question. "Yes, I'm married."

His wife's name? He replied, "Pubichet."

Now the doctor wanted to see if there could be any musical connection. He had already discovered in the life of Jack Carstairs, there had been a piano, where Chopin had been a favorite, and a small pump organ; there had been hymns but no discussion or sample of them from the friar, but oh, how much music and dance filled the life of the Tripolitan, just 100 years later than this one! Certainly there would be songs even in the chill semi-arctic.

"And when you married her, did your friends sing to you?"

"No."

"Do you have tribal songs? . . . and musical instruments?"

"No. It's too cold."

"You do not dance?"

"No."

That avenue was apparently closed. Either Gregor's group was not among the ones who had primitive instruments, or he did not consider those devices musical: The tribes are said to have had drum heads or tambourines which were used by a shaman, and accompaniment would be only by a small jew's harp of wood and metal, or a pipe of bone and reed.[3] Most Westerners would consider those mainly rhythmic, rather than musical.

Grim and cold, sparse and dreary, no music, no songs, in the life of Peter/Gregor. Was all of this man's life a struggle for bare survival?

The doctor decided to ask again about the language, as part of his plan to see if the subject would give the same answer each time or change it—indicating possible inconsistency. However, the question was misunderstood.

"I would like to have you greet us in your native tongue of Siberia."

The subject seemed to have heard "town" instead of "tongue."

"The town—Yukut. Yukut, 450 miles from Vladivostock. Ice, ice, ice all over."

"Yukut" was the way the typist heard the sound. "Yakut"—probably the way the word was actually pronounced—just happens to be the foremost of the Turkic type of Siberian ethnic groups. The Yakuts, according to the *Encyclopedia of*

Religion,[4] had migrated northward from southern Siberia, along the Lena River, and had settled in northeastern Siberia, "the coldest region in the world."

So Yakut might indeed be the name of their settlement, the place Gregor lived, just as there are many place names for ethnic groups elsewhere, such as Germantown, Chinatown, Irishtown (in Australia), Indian River, and more.

Earlier, Al had asked Dr. George to check any newly discovered lives for information relating to the spirit, manifestations in religion, worship, and beliefs. Now would be a good time to do that, for this theme had occurred in the other lives they had seen so far. But talking about "the spirit" had been different each time, in the other lives, as a chameleon would change color depending on its surroundings and the material it was resting on. A search for spiritual training had been part of Jack Carstairs's life, a vision of Jesus for the little French boy, some participation in Bible work in England, for James; even a life given over entirely to religion as the Italian friar—all showed it was highly likely to be a strong theme in this chill and sparse existence.

"What is your religion?"

"What's that?"

The hypnotist paused a second. Not even the observer recognized that word here? He would put it in other terms.

"What do you worship? What do you fear? Whom do you ask for help?" How could he make it any clearer?

The subject sighed. "Nothing. Nobody."

It was the hypnotist's turn to sigh.

"Do you not worship the elements?"

"Scared of wind."

Well, perhaps fear was a form of worship.

"What do you call the wind?"

"Vodslaw."

"What do you call the sun and moon and stars, and the earth?"

"Oii, blaa, kremla . . . God."

"In your native tongue you call the earth *what?*" Here was the word that in his present life Al associated with the great Lord of All, the word always spoken with reverence. Did he really call the earth . . .

"God," said Gregor.

God, thought the doctor. This life appeared the bleakest of all. Life in this cave-dwelling community was a life without joy, a life without light. More than the dark night of the soul—it was a cold, dark night.

Peter/Gregor found nothing in his icy existence here to correlate with the words "religion" and "worship." However, it is possible that if he were asked if he knew a shaman, his answer might have been different. The work of a shaman does not fit the usual religious categories.

"Yakut," as the foremost of the Turkic type of Siberian ethnic groups, does have a Yakut religion, in which "shamanism is a fundamental and striking feature of the Siberian culture," according to the *Encyclopedia of Religion.*[5] Shamanism is not itself a religion, but instead an amalgam of different rites and beliefs concerned with the different activities of the shaman—and, in fact, connected with different religious systems. The word *shaman,* in much use today, comes from Siberia through Russian sources from the Tunguz word *saman (xaman).* The shaman can help others in crises—if caused by spirits—and act as a mediator between this world and the other world for the soul. The soul itself has a dual nature, one soul confined in the body and a second part of the soul capable of leaving the body freely during sleep, trance, or sickness.

Gregor's home, probably among the Yukagir clan, would be with tribal people (exactly as he said), depending on deer hunting and reindeer breeding. It was the clan shaman who, as one of the leaders of the clan, would be its patron and keep the contact between the living and the dead—as well as the hunting rites. He would help clan members by curing diseases, keeping evil away, and by prophesying. Not what is generally associated with a minister of a Western church.

When we hear the strange conversation that Gregor shares at the end of this period, we may wonder if it was a shaman or a Master—or perhaps the latter within the former—who was speaking with him.

Since the Yakut religion was brought north from southern Siberia, probably only the more adaptable rites and rituals would stay with the tribes, because they would not have the supplies of trees and plants that were part of some of the southern ritual offerings. It was far simpler, in the tundra area, to see and fear the raw Vodslaw, rather than to recognize that there had been, in the southern origins, a goddess of the earth, who lives among beautiful birches and blesses the harvest.

The basic cosmology did consist principally of nature forms in a three-level universe, including the upper world of sky (that would include the sun, moon, and stars which the doctor mentioned), a middle world of humans and many spirits (who sometimes capture hunters' souls), and a lower world with evil spirits and a "sea of death." It is interesting that the name for this lower world is "allaraa," which means "below, downstream, in the north"—for the rivers of Siberia flow northward. Here, hell, as in Norse mythology, was cold. (We recall that hell, in warm countries, is considered hot.) So the cold in Gregor's bones must have been painful to his spirit as well.

The major natural force that Gregor feared was the wind. This follows the pattern of many races: the wind has been a god power in most early religions: Aeolus, the Greek and Roman wind-god, could bring victory or defeat to a fleet of ships by the way he blew; Thor, the storm god of the Norse, always brought wind with his thunder and could kill with thunderbolts; Zeus and his counterpart, Jupiter, could throw their own thunderbolts, and the wind would go with them. Even in the Judaeo-Christian religion, there is the well-known scene in which Elijah stood on the mountain and, as the Lord passed, the very first sign was "a great and strong wind" which shattered the mountain, followed by the earthquake, fire, and the "still, small voice."[6]

The doctor was musing on the apparent lack of a system of worship, when his subject spoke up: "Dandiwach, Dandiwach."

"What does 'Dandiwach' mean?"

"Hello." This time, the Siberian continued as if he were introducing himself to a foreigner: "Gregor, 820 A.D. Father's name is Gregorovitch. My name, Gregor."

Dr. George responded: "What does Gregor mean?"

The Siberian answered, "The world, the world. Simple name and does not seem to make any sense, and this old place full of ice doesn't seem to make any sense." It appears that the man who felt so much misery was experiencing an unusual philosophical mood. He continued, partly from the observer view: "Ice on the ground. So cold. It's 42° below zero." (The name Gregor, according to the dictionary, means "vigilant," from the Greek, *egeirein*, to awaken. Its second meaning, "to raise from the dead," is certainly significant for this Siberian personality.)

Dr. George had still another request of Al's he had promised to carry out: to ask his subject, at an appropriate point, if there was a motive, a meaningful pattern of some kind to his various lives. Would he be able, in the midst of these other geographic and physical contexts, to uncover one? If one was to come, what better place for a contrast than from a life where there was no recognition of religion as such, where the winds were the higher power, and cold was the permanent chain to earth?

He would ask the question. But first, he wanted to find out more about how this man met his death.

And perhaps, how such a miserable person had lived before.

"Where do you live?"

"In Yukut, underground."

"Why do you live underground?"

"It's too cold above ground."

Asked how he would say, "It's too cold," he started to talk about the language being "a peculiar language," then offered something the typist wrote as "Onecingdown," as "It's too cold."

Suddenly he turned as if seeing someone else. "'What are you doing here, Gregor?' somebody asks me."

"I got to work it out, I've got to work it out."

"Work out what?" the doctor questioned.

Gregor quoted the invisible person he was talking to: "Work out your karma. Gregor, don't you know that? You've got to go through this life with suffering. You've got to go through suffering. Jesus showed us the way, and you've got to do it, too. You've got to suffer." This voice spoke as a master would explain, directing—not angrily with rancor, but with compassion and understanding.

"'You're going to die, Gregor, you're going to die.'" This was not a threat, just a statement. The voice added, "It's 50° below zero."

The doctor and the witnesses could feel the chill. The doctor asked softly, "And do you die at 50° below zero?"

"Yes," came the quiet answer. "It was a good riddance of that body. It was tough." A sense of acceptance.

"And now you will rest. You will rest."

This was far enough for now.

It would be a reward for this soul to be born to live on the Mediterranean sands, to be filled with warmth, with sun, sand, and song, identifying the Maker of All with the sun and moon and stars. What a contrast to the pain of this one. Was it also a balance?

Where *had* he been before?

9
Life and Light

The man who had been the happy Tripolitan, the man who had been the sad Siberian, were one and the same. But two lives could hardly be more at polar opposites. The action of karma, loosely defined as the law of cause and effect, might be working here, but in what way? Dr. Henry George, as a researcher, was not looking at karma at all, but at what could be historically verifiable. Still, he could not help being interested in the life stories themselves, with their personal plots, triumphs, and tragedies. So it was with more than average interest that he again led Al back to the life as Achmesh, around 800 years before the Siberian died in the glacier rift.

He and the witnesses had already heard of the Roman life, by the seventh session, but because it seemed strongly influenced by part of Achmesh's life, we see the Hebrew first.

If *any* of the past lives needed deep exploration, it was this one back in the time of Christ. It had produced many facets, from birth to death, some highly emotional, some pragmatic, some grim.

Parts of the story Achmesh would tell from his own identity, parts from the observer viewpoint. They would explore from Achmesh's birth to his death, then plan to find out where the being went next. En route, Dr. George would bring up other data on the life of that period in Middle East history. He wanted as much information as possible before the linguist came.

He led the entranced subject back to the Jewish period.

"Who was king of Israel?"

"Israel had no king. Pontius Pilate ruled over Israel;[1] he was the governor. We were just subjects." Angry resentment underlined his words. "Slaves. Every time one of those Romans came, we had to hide. They had spears. They didn't hesitate to put them . . . I seen innocent Hebrew women with spears stuck in them just for sport! We were looking for a king to . . . deliver us from the Romans."

Whenever he mentioned the Romans, Achmesh spoke with wrath and scorn. The witnesses sensed his hatred under the surface. The Jews of that period were known to call the Romans "swine"—in part because the Roman soldiers carried banners displaying a tough fighting emblem—a picture of a wild boar.[2] And in part because that was the way these Jews felt about the foreigners who now ruled their country, according to Dr. Samuel Lachs, rabbi and retired professor of religion at Bryn Mawr College. This was the basis, the rabbi said, of Jesus' saying, "Cast not your pearls [of wisdom] before swine."

All right, so Israel had a governor instead of a king. Dr. George would see what he could find out from what the man Achmesh had already mentioned. "Tell us what you remember about Pontius Pilate."

"Bald headed."

Taken aback by the abrupt response, the doctor continued, "He was governor?"

"Yes. The only thing that distinguished him was his head." Achmesh's voice was sarcastic, bitter. "He didn't know anything. Just some monkey the emperor sent down." Achmesh enjoyed insulting the Romans.

"Who was emperor?"

Silence was a fit response. The average man in the street would have no contact with the emperor or—if he had his way—with any of the emperor's representatives. The first and best-known emperor, Caesar Augustus, had died in 14 A.D., when this Jew was about sixteen years old. Tiberius Claudius Nero Caesar, a Roman general nowhere near Augustus in genius or popularity, followed him as emperor until 37 A.D. The Roman way with colonies was to try to involve the people themselves in the lower orders of government to keep the populace from xenophobia, but the fierce nationalism that filled the land of Israel would make these collaborators extremely unpopular in Judaea. In fact, even speaking to or about them would arouse antagonism from the average Jew.

But Dr. George tried a different form of the question.

"Who was above the governor?"

"The emperor."

Now the doctor insisted on knowing: "Emperor who?"

"Nero."

Although known to history students today as Tiberius, the last name of the emperor then ruling *was* Nero, preceding the title of "Caesar." In contrast, the emperor known to posterity by the name, "Nero," was actually "Nero Claudius Caesar Drusus Germanicus," perhaps best known for playing his music during a fire while low-income housing burned.

Achmesh had pride in his background, in the tribe of

Benjamin. Although at first he simply gave the name of the tribe, in a later question he announced he was a "forty-first lineal descendant of Benjamin."

With a desire to show the family record, he said he was born in a town right next to Jacob's well. "My father's name was Elijah. He was named for Elijah the prophet; a lot of people were named Elijah." Achmesh gave two names for his mother: "Bath," which means "daughter of," and "Naomi."

When was he born? Of course, Achmesh himself had no idea of B.C. or A.D. Those terms were not in existence then. The answer would come from the "hidden observer" who could, as Dr. Fadiman[3] had explained, supply information, particularly when asked about dates, locations, or relationships. Achmesh then replied, "I was born 2 B.C. in a time of travail." Why was it a distressing time? "Everybody was scared, everybody was hiding. They were afraid of Herod. He was a monster."

"Why was he a monster?"

"Taxes . . . " Achmesh spoke with a rage not seen in any of the previous lives. "He was collecting everything in taxes and nobody had anything. If you didn't pay all you had in taxes, he left you nothing. That's all you had." But he needed to clear up an identity, so he explained, "There were two Herods, you know." (Herod the Great, king of Judaea from 37 B.C. to 4 B.C., was the father of Herod Antipas, who ruled from 4 B.C. to 39 A.D., and was the Herod Achmesh railed about.)

His occupation? When younger, he hauled water from the well for people to drink; later on, he was a carpenter, working mostly with stone tools, with stone and mortar.

Dr. George asked a question perhaps to test his subject—he would occasionally throw in a question which he knew was not fact (as he did with "James" when asking about steamboats). This question might also bring out a reaction to the name, "Judas."

"Judas had risen for the Israelites, and 900 of his men had been crucified." He paused, then, "Do you remember Judas? He was a hero. It was a little before the time of Pontius Pilate."

Silence. No response at all.

A search for historical men named Judas (the Greek form of Judah), from the son of Jacob to Judas Iscariot, turned up Judas, the brother of Jesus, plus Saint Judas, probably the apostle St. James, son of Alphaeus, not heard from after the ascension, according to the *Encyclopaedia Britannica*; also Judas Barsabas, a companion of Paul.[4] Much earlier was Judas Maccabaeus, who led a successful Jewish revolt against the Syrians in 175-164 B.C. Perhaps this one—nearly two hundred years *before* Achmesh—could be considered as a hero? But he did not fit the questioner's era: "A little before the time of Pontius Pilate." A century is far more than "a little," in this case. Small wonder there was silence. But he tried again.

"Did you ever hear of Spartacus, the Roman gladiator?" asked Dr. George.

Spartacus was actually a Thracian slave who led a revolt against the Romans, but was slain in 71 B.C.—69 years before this man was born.

It would be a wonder if Achmesh *had* heard of him.

"Can you speak to us as you would greet your friend?"

After his last outburst of bitterness and all these questions about people he didn't know and didn't want to know, Achmesh was not feeling friendly. "I am tired," was all he said.

"You are tired," Henry George agreed. "You have been on a long trip. Won't you share it with us?"

But the Hebrew said nothing.

Dr. George allowed this session to end, but made a note to look at that bitterness again.

The next time he began with Achmesh's childhood.

"Did you have happy boyhood memories?"

"No, didn't have nothin'."

"Did you have brothers or sisters?"

"Yeah, yeah, I had a sister. One sister."

"What were their names?"

"No," he corrected. "One sister. One sister." Impatience was showing. "Her name—you can't say it. (Sounded like) Nacnacima . . . Nacnacima. I don't know where they got that name."

"Was she older or younger than you?"

"She was five years older than I. She was born 7 B.C." (The "observer" was keeping the dates straight according to our present calendar.)

"Was she a pretty girl?"

"I don't know." A typical brotherly remark. "When she was twenty, I was fifteen. And she was deaf. Oh, she used to go to the well there . . . She used to go to the well to get water and take it in to Jerusalem."

Because Al had previously asked to learn if any of the people in his previous lives were known to him in the present, Dr. George chose this point to ask, "Do you see your sister in any friend about you?" This, of course, called for an "observer" who could be out of the Hebrew identity yet recalling it and observing the present life at the same time.

It happened:

"Wait a minute, yes. That Wilmer Alice Adams I just met was Nacnacima. That's the only person. I just met her, too—Goodness!"

The doctor pursued this line, again aiming the question at the man between lives. "Do you remember anyone else whom you now know—or have known?"

"Judy Chandler, at Virginia Beach. I met her once."

"Who was she?"

The "observer" murmured, "I'm tired. That was a tremendous experience, a lifetime. Oh . . . " he sighed deeply, then responded:

"She was . . . a teacher at Mount Carmel."

It was difficult for Dr. George to control his desire to get more data on this vital life, but he encouraged the sleeper to rest . . . "and keep the happy family memories."

Suddenly the subject seemed to get a rush of energy and memory at the same time: "That's who she was, yes! That's who she was. She was the woman at the well!"

"Tell us again?" The hypnotist was taken aback.

"Oh, no!" Al was startled by the discovery of a quotation that fit: "You know . . . 'And there was a man and he told me I had five husbands!'[5] No, you'd never . . . that's who my *sister* was! It's too much. I can't talk about it. It's too big. Some other time, please." He was more than surprised, he was overwhelmed.

Now Dr. George understood Achmesh's reluctance to say more. "You protect that, that's your secret. That's your right . . . "

"It's too big, it's too important." The voice was pleading.

Dr. George offered comforting words as his subject gradually relaxed, muttering "Very tired."

It was June 29, 1952, when they had the session at the A.R.E. headquarters in Virginia Beach. Here, Dr. George hoped to reveal crucial material about this peculiarly stressed and pivotal life.

Here, as new witnesses Hugh Lynn Cayce, David Kahn, Gladys Davis, and her friend watched, Dr. George directed Al to go back "to your life as Achmesh and describe for us the most vivid moment, the greatest experience of this life."

After a couple of long, slow breaths, a tense silence. Then words tumbling after each other:

"Noise, thunderstorm, tremendous noise, awful earthquake! What are all those people doing?!"

Asked to describe them, he impatiently protested, "Can't you see them? They're all filthy!" He was somehow in a different mode, no longer speaking as the Hebrew *man* but as a horrified young observer, another in the "nest of selves" Dr. Fadiman had mentioned, calling out as a twentieth-century boy might describe what he saw back then. "Bedouins, some kind of dirty people, nightgowns on, one-piece nightgowns."

"Were they clean-shaven?"

"No, they all have beards, filthy, dirty, rotten filth, all running, running, running. They're scared of something!" He was feeling panic. "Storm, thunder, lightning, earthquakes. Do you hear it? There's a lot of people rushing by me, knocking me down. I get up again. Oh, what noise, deafening noise, thunder. No wonder the people are scared and running. I just stood there. Couldn't move, couldn't move because I was faced the other way."

"And why were you faced the other way?"

"I was looking at a man, and he was being crucified."

"How did they crucify him?"

"They ran away and left him there. Big cross, oak wood. All the people have left him, everybody left. I'm a little ways away. I can hardly see." He was trembling on the couch.

"You can bring it up," the doctor encouraged.

"Exquisite agony." No longer the boy, the mode had changed; the man, no longer panicky, but seeing the horror. "Has blood running from his right eye."

To the doctor's question, was he wounded in the eye, he answered, "No, I can't understand it. The spear . . . the right side, there's a hole there big enough for your finger, two fingers. Powerful arms strung to that cross. Physically they are so powerful they could have torn the cross down. There are three crosses there. There are two smaller ones. Hill of Golgotha. Stream along there. I'm kind of frozen. I can't move away or forward. I can't move. I can't move."

The man on the couch held himself stiff.

"Why is this so significant?" the doctor probed. "You have seen men crucified before."

"Lots of times, but something's happening here, there's something happening I can't understand. What makes everybody run away? What makes all that thunder and the earthquakes?" He paused, listening. "A voice. A lady's there. She came from nowhere. The man. The voice said, 'Woman, behold thy son,' and 'It is finished.' Everybody's gone except that woman and him. I don't know who they are. I don't know. I'm a long ways away. It is very far. I want to . . . so much, I want to see, I can't move. I want to see who that is . . . " he mumbles. "Voice says it's Jesus."

"And who is Jesus?" Henry George asks.

"King of the Jews."

"Did you know him?"

Scarcely breathing: the witnesses listened as he answered:

"I met him once at the well . . . My sister went there for water. But I didn't know they were putting him on a cross! I don't know what that's for, or why all this noise, dirty, filthy people wandering around me. They're gone now." His face and muscles relaxed. "Thank you, Jehovah. Now there's no one there."

"They've taken him away?"

"He's gone."

Quickly Dr. George decided to try to record some language if he could, before another identity might show up.

"Would you say some words for us in your native tongue?"

The typist records speaking, but does not transliterate.

"And will you tell us what that is?"

"Aramaic."

Now the doctor realized he should have asked, *what does that mean*, but he continued, "What is the Aramaic language, and what does it mean?"

Apparently Dr. George was, like many others today, unaware of Aramaic. It was at one time the common language of the Near East; indeed, according to Gerrit Judd,[6] it had been formerly "The international language of trade" during the days of the Assyrian Empire and a half-millennium after. In the first century A.D., however, while Latin was the chief commercial language, Aramaic—very similar to Hebrew—was the common language all around that area and was the language spoken by Jesus and his disciples.[7]

As before, when the hypnotist had asked two questions together, the subject answered only the second question. He talked about his sister meeting this man at the well, the man who told her she had already had five husbands. It seems the man had a quality about him that made her understand him, even though she had been deaf. The subject added, as a somewhat shocked younger brother, "I didn't know that—and she was my sister!" His sister had run back home and told her family, "The man at the well told me all that I ever knew!"

Achmesh added, "And I met him that time, but I didn't know who he was. He was the man on the cross who was crucified."

"Did you become a follower of this man?"

"No, no! I didn't know what all this was about." When Al spoke as Achmesh, he spoke usually from a particular time in his life—this particular time from the day his sister ran home with the news of the encounter at the well. Later he learned many of Jesus' teachings. But when he was watching the cross, he couldn't move: "I was afraid of all those Roman soldiers."

"What did the Roman soldiers do?"

Now the perception shifted to the broadly felt anti-Roman bias: "Sharp swords and spears, and if they found anyone who tried to break away from the Roman yoke, they just speared him. So I stayed away."

Now, he spoke from a later perspective. "The people talked after this of Christians. I met some of them, I never became one."

To round out the picture, the doctor asked, "What did you

do with the rest of your life? How did you work? How did you support yourself?"

"Carpenter."

"Would you describe the tools that you used?"

"Hammer of stone. We had a stone saw, and we used sand (and a mix) to put rocks together. Hammer, stone chisel, stone saw."

"Did you work mostly on stone rather than on wood?"

"On stone. There's lots of wood . . . but I just work with stone."

VISIT TO NAZARETH

Then came the night Dr. George called on someone well versed in the Hebrew language to check out this religiously crucial lifetime: Mr. Heber Nelson, who had a knowledge of Hebrew. He also brought in the new friend Al had mentioned in the last session, Wilmer Alice Adams, and Mrs. Hadassah Roberts. These and other members of the Theosophical Society met in Dr. George's Wilmington office, the evening of July 1.

This time when Al had entered the Jewish lifetime, after he sighed heavily, he said one word:

"Nazareth."

"What about Nazareth?"

"I'm in a synagogue, with a dome."

"And what is the date?"

Here, naturally, the observer would speak, giving the date, even trying to explain the address:

"Five A.D. X-11 is the number, the street is Untwine, Nazareth." Now he spoke in character. "I'm seven years old. It's hot. Sand. The street is sand. I'm going in the synagogue. Oh, there's a lot of noise. Doves flying around. People shouting. I don't like this place."

Asked to describe it, he continued, but as the observer,

not as the seven year old: "It is marble, which comes from Lebanon, with marble steps. There are people jostling each other. There is a man with a beard six inches long. It's light and dark brown, light brown around his chin, and then it's dark brown. His name is David, lineally descended from David, King of Israel. David Xerthes. He wants to talk to me."

"You speak with him."

"He wants to talk to me, he says" (the typist tried to write the sounds: "Ta ta won la") "and I say that I don't like the place. I'm going out of it. And I walked out. It makes me sick to see all these people jostling each other. Then I walk down the steps and go back to my mother."

He continues as the child: "We have a tent. Oh, what a pretty tent! It's got six strings on it! 'Shalom, Mama.' "

Heber Nelson speaks: "Shalom."

"Is that you, Mama?" His mama did not have a baritone voice.

"It is a friend." Dr. George assures him.

Mr. Nelson speaks again in Hebrew.

"Who is it, Mama? Where are you, Mama? I don't know who that is!" As a seven year old meeting an unexpected stranger in his home, he would naturally be alarmed.

"It is a friend," Henry George soothes him again. "You will speak with your friend. He will greet you and you will speak. You will hear his greeting, and you will speak."

Heber Nelson speaks in Hebrew.

Achmesh replies in something that sounds like Hebrew. (With no recording available of this session, we have only the written transcript to go by.)

Again, Mr. Nelson speaks and Achmesh replies. This happens twice more, but then Achmesh does not answer. Henry George reassures him, as one would a child, "You will answer; he is your friend."

Heber Nelson tries again.

Achmesh replies, "Who?"

With a mild rebuke, Dr. George says, "You have a friend who is speaking in your tongue and you will answer him."

"I'm too young. I don't know him. Maybe when I get a little older I'll understand."

"That is well."

Plaintively, the "boy" continues, "I'm seven years only. I'm going to take lessons. My mama tells me I should know the language. I'm going to study."

It is not surprising that Achmesh feels inadequate and unhappy here. It would be logical for Mr. Nelson to be speaking in *ancient Hebrew,* as a language he had studied, but for Achmesh, the *common Aramaic* would be the everyday speech, not the Hebrew of the priests and scholars. It is not likely he would easily recognize Mr. Nelson's words, any more than a seven-year-old boy from Brooklyn would understand the speech of a London scholar.

(When Al or Mr. Nelson is later said to be speaking Aramaic or speaking Hebrew, the choice of language comes from the original typist's manuscript and was doubtless indicated by Henry George on the basis of probability, not by proof that it was one language or the other. The linguist never said it wasn't.)

Henry George resumed the search.

"Now tell us about your mother. What is her name?

"Her name is Naomi, Bath . . . "

The doctor interrupts to cross-check: "Do you have any brothers or sisters?"

The boy repeats that he has a sister named Nacnacima. "We're going to go to school, though, and learn under Rabbi Tine. He has the synagogue at Bethel, but I want to see my mama now in the tent, and she isn't there." The seven year old sounded nervous, not wanting to offend these adults. His mama was not there, and someone with a strange voice was speaking to him. He needed to find his mama. "I think she went to wash clothes at the water. Oh, there she is!"

Now, a fresh chance for dialogue. "You greet your mother," the doctor orders.

"Mama!" A happy child's cry. ("Mama" is the child's name for his mother in most European languages, also ancient Latin and Greek. But a very similar sound is "Ima" [or "eema"], the Hebrew and Aramaic word for mother.)

"And how does your mother greet you?"

The subject seemed to slide into another setting, another time.

"Sunset. Fifteen years old. I'm living in the town of Judasat. It was here Solomon came to arrange with many carpenters."

"And what are you doing here?"

"Trying to read the Aramaic inscription on the front of the synagogue."

"You will bring that up and read it to us."

"It says . . . (He reads the first, second, and third word; the typist writes: 'Lama xertes xertes,' then) . . . The fourth word is a long one. Hmm . . . (he mutters something) and the fifth word is just O and the sixth word (he spells) JHVH."

Heber Nelson asks, "What does JHVH mean?"

"Jehovah in your language. Jehovah, Lord God of Israel. Synagogue. Look, Look, can't you see him? Rabbi . . . Oh, isn't he beautiful?"

"Describe him to us."

"Thin, beard, very thin hair, red hair. Goodness, he's got a halo around him. I can see it. And his hair is like fire, as though it's on fire."[8]

"What is his name?"

"It's Rabbi Tine."

"Will you greet him?"

" 'Shalom, Master.' I don't want to go away from him. He's dressed in black, but he seems so ethereal, beautiful." Here Achmesh is a fifteen-year-old, with some scholarly training beyond the common Aramaic; he appears to speak in Hebrew. "He's speaking to me. I kneel at his feet." Again, the

Hebrew speech. "I can't speak to him; he's too holy. The words over his head stand out: JHVH. I kneel in humbleness, speechless. There's a . . . comes to me . . . It's written in the sand . . . Sand, and there's the sun coming up. Oh!" He is ecstatic. "Oh! Ah! Oh! Wait a minute . . . " Now he is panting, incoherent with joy.

Achmesh, now a teen-ager, is not the angry Hebrew castigating the Romans; he seems lit up with happiness.

"Can you tell us what is happening?" Dr. George asks.

"Oh, a whole lot of things."

Three times Dr. George pleads, then orders him to tell what is happening.

"Somebody is there. A whole lot of people following him."

"Following who?"

"I don't know who it is. Some man, red hair. Oh, look at that red hair. Funny, I can see him right next to me almost, and yet he's way, way off and all these people are following him." It sometimes happens under hypnosis that a person sees something of significance at a distance; then, as if with a zoom lens, sees it really close up. Al had this experience when he first saw the man on the center cross. The writer had a similar experience under hypnosis in 1983.

Al is still panting. "Can't seem to catch up. Let me run awhile, I'll catch up. I don't know; there are too many people. Wait a minute. I'm getting closer. Shadow of a cross on the hill, a large shadow. Must be a thousand people, and on the other side is the sea of Galilee." Here he speaks in Hebrew again. "Multitudes of people. Thousands of them all over. I don't know what it's all about. Jesus . . . "

Heber Nelson interrupts, speaking in Hebrew.

The subject replies with words that include "Dua Achmesh" and more in Hebrew. He starts panting. "I've got to run awful fast. He's left. He got in a boat. All the people are standing, watching. Some are on crutches—then jumping up and down! Some fellow . . . he's pulling up corn and throwing it all over, he's so happy. He's throwing it way up in the air!"

"What is he throwing?"

"Corn. Can't you see it? He's got a whole lot and he's happy." Few of the witnesses were aware that "corn" is, in the King James Version of the Bible, a word for wheat or the grain of any cereal plant; that is the British meaning of "corn," not the American meaning of the grain of the plant known as maize.

Asked what year it was, he replied:

"Thirty-two A.D. The date is by the Julian calendar, XIV. I'm stopped . . . July 14, 32 A.D." The observer, not Al, would know about the Julian calendar, which was the "new" calendar established by Julius Caesar in 46 B.C., with 365 days each year and an extra day added every fourth year. This attempted to correct the original Roman calendar, where a couple of days "off" each year had let the spring months slip back to winter. It, of course, had no indication for A.D. at that time. XIV was the Roman numeral fourteen, but not the way they would indicate July 14. That would be "PR. ID. JUL." or "day before the Ides of July."

"Something happened here today. It's still happening," Achmesh said. "Maybe I can catch a boat. Oh, there's another one gone. No more boats. I can swim. Yeah, yeah, the water's cold . . . It's not far."

"What is not far?"

"The other side. It's a lake . . . called the sea of Galilee. I'm stuck!" He seemed to have gotten out of the water. "Oh, it feels good to lie down on the sand." He is panting.

"Rabbi, Rabbi . . . Somebody's calling . . . that man. They call him Jesus and . . . " His voice broke as he struggled with his feelings . . . "Oh, I can't stand it to be near him! It's ecstasy! It's too much!" He gulped. "I'm just a mild fellow. It's too much for me . . . frightening!" His whole body was reliving the experience.

Achmesh continued with tremendous emotion, describing the people calling out "Rabbi," but adding, "He's not a rabbi. I know he's not a rabbi, he's—a carpenter!

"He's gonna talk. All those people come over in a boat; they're sitting down. Maybe I can hear him, but I'm awful far away. I want to get up closer. I don't know where all those people come from. He crossed the lake and here are these people on the other side. Like sheep."[9] Then, "He's gonna talk!"

ACHMESH REPEATS A SERMON BY THE SEA

Ye have heard that it hath been said by them of olden time, "thou shalt not kill, or thou shalt be in danger of the judgment," but I say unto you every man who is angry with his brother shall be in danger of the judgment, and whosoever shall say to his brother, "Raca, Raca," shall be in danger of the council.[10] Whosoever shall say to his brother, "Thou fool," (here he appears to speak in Aramaic) . . . Ye are hungry, give me of that which you have and I will feed you. Peter, how much bread have we? Fifteen loaves. Give it to all the people and they shall eat. Give me the one fish and I will break bread with you and ye shall drink of my blood that ye too may be one, even as I am one with the Father; that thou art.

It is twilight. Ye have eaten, now eat ye of the spiritual bread that our Father giveth. I and my Father are one. What ye now have is better than that ye would have, for the purpose in a man's heart is that to be one with me. I am the life, the light, the lead, the bread, the world life. Come only unto the Father through me. It is said by them of olden times, "The Ten Commandments must be kept," but I give unto you a new Commandment: "Love one another." As twilight deepens, rest . . . rest in the arms of your heavenly Father.

Dr. George and the witnesses were in rapt silence. But the subject shifted his focus to an entirely different scene. He described being under "trees with white tops" and wondered how he came there, then spoke Aramaic (according to the typist). "That's where Solomon got his trees. I feel that I must have known him," he finished.

But Dr. George wanted to get back to the preacher.

"Tell us more about this carpenter, this carpenter who preaches."

"You mean . . . ?"

"Jesus."

"The Nazarene?

"That Nazarene."

That golden moment of time had gone past. Dr. George did not pick up the mention of Solomon.

"I don't know where he is. I'll try to find him . . . First, got to go back. Fifteen A.D." An observer is ready to search through time.

Cooperating, Henry George told the sleeping man, "You're going back to 15 A.D."

"(To) 15 A.D. . . . Can you imagine that! Judy Chandler. Mount Carmel—That's where he (Jesus) is now. (She is) teaching him the mysteries. Fifteen years old. I don't see him. He is learning. Judy Chandler is teaching. He is fifteen, but I don't seem to be going there."

"Who is Judy Chandler?"

"She now is in Virginia Beach in 1952."

Dr. George wants the information from the dual views of Achmesh and the observer. "But what is her character?"

"Her name is Ruth . . . like the Book of Ruth, and she's teaching the mysteries at Mount Carmel. And Jesus is fifteen. But they won't let me up, no, they won't let me up the hill. They won't let me come in," he protests. "All kinds of things to prevent anyone. Do you want to know what they are?"

The observer describes a thick stand of trees at the base of the Mount, and a row of monks guarding the area half-way up, because of an important event going on. It could be that Jesus is being taught the mysteries. "They won't let me up!" he protests.

The observer goes forward in time as he tries to locate Pontius Pilate, finds him, gives a detailed description of his jewelry, robe, sandals, and more. This time, Pilate is wearing the Star of David on a crown.

"He ain't got a title to it" is the ungrammatical comment. Al never used poor grammar in his current life. "He sits in judgment. He says he can do anything."

Achmesh continues, " 'Art thou the King of the Jews?' he asks Jesus, and Jesus said, 'Thou hast said it.'"

"What do the people say?"

"Crucify him! Crucify him!" The speaker didn't want to stop. "Crucify him! Crucify him! Crucify him! . . . "

Henry George wanted to know, "How do the people say that?"

(The words sounded like) "Lanz! Lanz! Lanz!" Later he gives a Latin cry for the same purpose.

" 'Take him away. I wash my hands of the whole business,' says Pontius Pilate. I don't want to talk about it any more." The subject gave a short cry, then a startled "Good night!" but when asked what he had seen, said, "It is not to be given."

Perhaps to compensate for that refusal, Achmesh's observer offered to give them information about the birth of Jesus. Obviously, Achmesh, born about the same time, could not have made the description. The observer describes three men, Zoroastrians, and speaks in another language. (Unfortunately the tape of this section is missing, but Dr. George's typist wrote "Persian.") He describes these three men meeting "directly east of Bethlehem," then coming to the cave where the birth took place. "The child was born at 2:01 in the morning." He makes a sound the typist describes as "a wail like a newborn's cry," then says the cave will be discovered in 1952. He lists many items he says will be found in it, including sandals, coins, and a stone jar.

In addition there is a stone hatchet. He comments, "Who put that there? It doesn't belong there. For the rule of Jesus is love. Love conquers all. Somebody placed it there . . . it must have been a Mohammedan, later on."

Later, he gives many more details of the cave, its measurements, the structure of the roof, repaired many times. The roof is iron, "that was put there 400 A.D. to protect the birthplace. All I can think of is the cross. There is no cross here, it is just felt. Omnipresent."

The doctor is quite interested in details; Achmesh's observer lists more objects to be found in it, including a flat piece of tin shaped like a triangle. Dr. George asks for the composition of the tin; the observer says: "3.265 percent copper. There is 2.166 percent antimony, 90.65 percent tin, the remainder is just a mixture." (Al was not known to have any metallurgical training or experience.)

Then he picks up other items: a wooden pillow made of cedar, two broken candlesticks of gold with handles. He is about to continue when Henry George interrupts the museum-type descriptions:

"We are grateful for the identifications you have given us, and now will you go back into the personality of Achmesh and tell us how you saw the crucifixion?"

CRUCIFIXION, CRISIS, AND SYMBOLS

"March second, 35 A.D. That's not the date that's recognized but here is the fact." The speaker says he is picking up pink hyacinths that someone dropped. The hyacinth, in Greek mythology, was created by Apollo in sorrow for the death of a beloved young man.

The speaker sees, hears, and describes a crowd: “Filthy, there are bugs on them, oh, they are dirty, one hasn’t washed in years, scrofulous, no good . . . they are all running, running! They are running, scared of the thunder, the lightning, the wind. They are scared of the man . . . Up on the cross; they have crucified him. It seems as though the cross is magnified many times.” As noted earlier, this magnification or “zoom” effect occurs sometimes during hypnotic observation. “There is a cross on each side; there is a crown of thorns that somebody wanted to attach, but they dropped it. The cross is eight feet tall; he carried it. He’s bleeding.

“ ‘Father, forgive them; they know not what they do.’

“They are all running—he scared them even more. Blood is gushing from his right eye. His eyes are closed . . . long lashes. I can see this well a long way away. There are two nails in his right hand and one nail and a rusty nail in his left. Right at the calf, right through the calf of each leg there is a huge spike. Blood is coming out from his eye but no blood from the hands where the nails are. The cross is made from a kind of oak wood. Everybody is running, running . . . why don’t they go away and leave me alone?”

It becomes very quiet. He sees the man, Nicodemus, coming up. His emotions are real.

“Shalom, Nicodemus; it is your friend Achmesh.”

At once Dr. George asks him, “Will you please say that in your native tongue?”

He does. The typist wrote: “He responds in a foreign tongue.”

“He recognizes me. He came to take this man down. I said, ‘Why do you bother with him?’ He said, ‘It is Jesus.’ I said, ‘What difference does it make?’ He said, ‘It is Jesus, it is Jesus.’ I didn’t know, I didn’t know that I knew Jesus. I met him but I didn’t know who he really was.”

The agony was palpable. Suddenly he broke out in Hebrew.

"What does that mean?" asked the doctor. "Eloi, Eloi?"

"'My God, my God!' . . . then the earth shook. Rain, tremendous rain." He described Nicodemus ignoring the rain, lifting up the cross, laying it down gently, gently taking Jesus, wrapping him . . . taking him to the tomb that he had prepared. Mary was there, the speaker added, but she wouldn't go along.

ACHMESH RECALLS JESUS' TEACHINGS

"Were you a follower of Jesus?"

"No, I was just there," Achmesh replied. "He was a nice man, kind, a friend."

"What did he teach?"

"Love. He taught that the sky and the earth were one, that there was a spirit, far above the mind of man; that spirit was God, and all things were made by Him. He with Jesus created this world—I thought that did not make any sense—The Father gave him, the son, that with which to create, and he did.

"He taught that through love everyone should give up their life as He would, and by giving up their life they would find it. When it was given up, it was submerged in that which was, is, and will be . . . He taught that as one will, he can become as one with all being. Matter, energy, all were one—and he, Jesus, would prove it . . . that life and inert matter were the same . . ." (This very same concept was the central theme of a lecture by Dr. William Tiller in the series by the Center for Frontier Sciences of Temple University, Philadelphia, on September 28, 1993. Dr. Tiller cited experiments and events that pointed to the same thing—that consciousness is in all matter.)

Achmesh reiterated that Jesus taught that "every person alive should become as one with every other person, and that the Lord and He were one, and nothing is separate. But only through free will may man lose that which he has, and not just what he has but his life; he can never find it unless he loses it."

John Donne (1573-1631) said it well: "No man is an island, entire of itself; every man is a piece of the continent . . . I am involved in all mankind." This philosophy is rarely recognized by leaders and thinkers today, although it is examined by a few like Dr. Tiller. No wonder it was a heavy problem for the witnesses and Dr. George.

"But you did not believe this," Dr. George said as the tense Achmesh finished trying to communicate the complex thoughts.

"It is too much for me. I don't understand it," he admitted.

THE STONING OF STEPHEN

Al went ahead to another scene before the final one:

"I am on a road and it is dusty. There are a lot of people, maybe fifteen people, and they are stoning a man."

"Who are they stoning?"

"Stephen. It is awful.

"He wore a belt, red and gold; and he followed and preached the Master, Stephen told me after that crucifixion. And I saw him stoned. He said, 'Achmesh, carry this message: Christ is king, and, Achmesh, you will get exactly what I get.' " Even in the trance his voice was stressed, his face was strained.

"Did you rise to Stephen's defense?" Henry George asked gently.

"Too late. I got there too late." Achmesh the man was in the middle of a melee, taking part in it and telling about it at the same time. "Stephen, Stephen!—Saul, what are you doing here? Get away, he is my friend Stephen!—They are throwing stones at him! Saul is doing it!" Then he was describing Stephen: “He’s beautiful, he’s dying. Beautiful blue eyes, but he’s bleeding all over. They won’t stop throwing stones. He could have got better, but they wouldn’t stop. ‘Get away, Mesaah!’ ” he told the watchers. “Saul says he’s got orders to stone Stephen and tells *me* to get away. I tried to hold him, but he’s stronger than I.” The man on the couch showed anguish. “They are done stoning him now; he’s still got the gold and red belt around him, but it’s torn.

“They are going away now, there is just Stephen and I. ‘Stephen, Stephen!’ He’s looking up now. His face is just a mash of blood. I can hardly see his eyes for blood is falling into them. There’s a gash two inches above his left eye and blood is streaming out of it. There are stones all around. He’s going to speak.

“‘Father, forgive them.’ That’s all he says . . .”

The witnesses wanted to comfort the grieving man, but Dr. George asked him, “Will you say that in your native tongue?” and Al spoke some syllables, then lay back, panting. Gradually he grew calmer.

“Do you know Saul?” Henry George went on. “Tell us about him.”

“Big man,” the subject said, “Six foot one-and-one-half inches tall. Solid black hair, with a ring in his hair, knotted. He has a grimace—he’s always grimacing, thinks he can scare people by making an ugly face. He’s a big bruiser with black, matted eyebrows. He wears a yellow cloak that’s supposed to be for gold and underneath is purple of royalty. He’s a great man to these people, persecuting the Christians, killing them. But I can see his soul—he’s hungering and thirsting and crying out. His soul is tortured.” At the end he added: “He’s got a spear eight feet long made of bronze, the tip is silver. He’s powerful.”

There was quiet for a moment.

“And as Stephen died, I held him in my arms, and then I saw Jesus again . . . but it wasn’t the same. He was actually there—but he wasn't there. This was ten years after he was crucified. And I had to do that, then, to carry on Stephen's message.

"What a wonderful way to die, I thought." By this point, they could see that Achmesh had changed his view, his feelings about Jesus. "Stephen and Jesus forgave. I thought he was the Christ everyone looked for, and they crucified him for it.

"What more could anyone want than that? Many of us, many of us. They crucified everyone right and left. Paul they crucified upside down, finally."

"And what was your fate? How did you meet your end?"

"The same way." He drew a breath. A strange smile came on his face. "Glory! Glory. They crucified me, too."

"Where?"

"In Judaea; 61 A.D."

"You were crucified . . . and what was your offense?"

"Light. I saw that this man was the Christ, and I believed it, and they crucified many for that offense, for believing in Him. But I was just one of many, happy for the opportunity."

"Who caught you?"

"I don't know. They crucified me. That was when Saul was meeting Dorcas."

"Had he become an apostle?"

"No. She was going to try him and test him. In this body I don't know what happened, 'cause they caught me."

"Who tried you?"

"They didn't *try* me," Achmesh clarified, "they just caught me and crucified me. They didn't try any of us."

"It was not by order of the Sanhedrin?"

"The Sanhedrin ordered it, but they just went wild; they went way past the Sanhedrin's orders. They said everyone should be brought before the Sanhedrin and tried. They didn't try me."

"Were you executed by the Romans or by the Jews?"

"By the Jews."

This—*this* was the man who feared the Roman soldiers? This man who cried, "Glory, glory," at the recollection of his own death? But there are emotional highs that some people have experienced, a complete transcendence of the physical that can bring to martyrdom a form of rapture. Al was feeling and acting these experiences as Achmesh, knowing them as an observer.

"What government did this?"

The subject lay silent.

"Will there be any records of Achmesh?"

He answered, "The records were placed in the tomb of Jesus, of Achmesh, and Stephen."[11]

"Now you rest," Dr. George urged softly. "You will rest."

But a picture was forming in the sleeper's mind.

"The light! The light—in the tomb of Jesus, where they keep the records."

"Have they found this tomb?"

"No, it is not to be given. The light!—It's all light and always will be . . . " His voice faded.

10
Captain Slaughter

The Latin word *strages* (pronounced *strah-gace)* means a pile of debris, havoc, massacre, slaughter.

In the seventh session, Dr. George had again brought Al back to the time he spoke as Achmesh, the Hebrew; he told of his encounters with Stephen and with Saul, who at that time was still working furiously to stamp out the followers of Jesus.

But there was a gap, a gap of nearly 800 years between the life of Achmesh and the life of the Siberian cave dweller, Peter/Gregor. What happened after the end of the Hebrew's life, which held the mind-blanking experience of the crucifixion? The hypnotist would try to fill it in.

"And now if you will leave the experience of Achmesh, and search out and find where next your individuality incarnated, and will you tell us about it?"

This did not take long. Soon, a shift in breathing, and Al was ready to speak.

"The year 201 A.D. The name—'Stronges' (as the typist wrote it). This name would be pronounced "strahn-gace" in classical Latin. The closest Roman approximation to that name appears to be the Latin word pronounced "strah-gace," spelled "strages," meaning "massacre"[1] or "slaughter." That is not only a similar sound but, judging from what this man was soon to say, quite appropriate. We know the name came from somewhere in Al's mind, a mind which had picked up on such unlikely names as "Yakut" and "Ugric," which fit precise places in Siberian history. If we look at the derivation of the English word "strong," we find it traced through Anglo-Saxon to Old Norse, *strangr*, related to German *streng*, meaning "severe," and an older base meaning of "tense or taut." This does go back to the Latin "stringere"—"to pull tight or draw taut." And certainly this captain had reason enough to be tense! However, the Latin meaning of *strages* as "slaughter" is equally fitting, considering how he handled his enemies in battle. And the secondary meaning of "debris" fits the way he treated his women friends and children, before meeting Brunhilde.

In the trance, Strages spoke brusquely: "Born a bastard, from the pope. I'm an illegitimate son of the pope. My mother's name, Delas (day-las)." ("Delas" might be a feminine of *Delos*, the name for the Greek island of prophecy.)

This could be a rare life to investigate, but some witnesses' eyebrows were already raised at the idea of a bastard son of a pope. That would mean he would have to be Christian, wouldn't it? Then again, if he was not acknowledged by his father—which he wasn't (he said he never saw the man)—he could have been of the state religion. Wasn't Christianity a very small minority group in the third century? Had it spread so much in 150 years or so from the apostle Peter, often called its founder? Could it truly be that safe a religion in the Roman Empire before Constantine? It was in conflict with the state religion, the traditional polytheism, even though no one paid more than respectful political lip service to the gods.

But it was hardly likely that a Roman soldier who admitted—almost bragging—that he was the pope's son, could be applying that religion to his life at this point.

Christianity, in the popular mind, did not really surge in strength until the Emperor Constantine's conversion in 312 A.D. when—after praying to Christ for victory, then winning a battle—he ordered the Roman Empire to take Christianity as the state religion.

More light on the subject, however, shows that Christians had been gaining ground steadily, from the time Saul of Tarsus was converted, around 35 A.D. It was then he took the name Paul and went with his knowledge of Greek, Latin, and history and his energetic speeches to the Greek and Roman cities along the Mediterranean. These new Christian groups he was helping were considered an underground, subversive cult movement by many Roman politicians, as well as by Jews. But they kept growing.

During the lifetime of this man whom we'll call Strages—and since he was an army captain, "Captain Slaughter" seems to fit—the Roman Empire was no longer the marble grandeur and prosperous society it had been under the first emperor, Augustus. Rome's resources were running out; it faced an economic depression. During the third century (from 201, the year of Strages's birth), "the empire entered a dreary period of crisis and decline."[2] When Strages was born, the emperor was an African, Lucius Septimius Severus, who set up a strong military despotism. Politics and civil government went by the military rule. In the next century there were well over two dozen soldier-emperors, all calling themselves, what else? "Caesar."

Despite the confusion, there were still considerable benefits from the Roman civilization which set the areas of the Empire far above the barbarians. One, of course, was the literacy—there was a higher percentage of people in the empire able to read and write than any time in the future—until the *nineteenth* century![3] Another was the Roman roads—one of the outstanding achievements of the ancient world. Some in southern countries are still in use today, constructed so skillfully that they even went beyond the road-building standards of nineteenth-century United States.[4] They stretched to the frontiers of the empire, through Europe, to Britain, even Syria. These roads made it possible for the Roman soldiers to march farther and move more equipment than those of any other country.

Perhaps due in part to the Roman roads, there was rising strength among the Christians, who had developed branches run by bishops. The word bishop comes from the Greek word *episcopos* meaning "overseer." The head bishop in charge of several groups was called "Papa" from the Greek *pappa*, familiar form of father. We know that today the Italian word for the pope is still "Il Papa."

Now, the doctor wanted to know, "Who was the pope, your father? What was his name?"

"Cleomentho," was the answer. "Illegitimate son . . . he had lots of them. He had lots of women." It was almost like bragging. (Clement was a name meaning "merciful," given to a saint who lived during the time of Paul, and believed to be the first with the title "Papa" or pope, but Clement was also the name—during Strages's time—of an important Greek Christian. It was a popular name for popes, in fact fourteen of them. The most recent, Clement XIV, lived 1769-1774.)

There is another aspect to this papal data. The now-revered title of Pope or Papa, according to the *Britannica Micropedia,* in the second and third centuries was given out quite freely—to *any* bishop and sometimes to simple priests. Whether or not it was really the title of the father of Strages, it certainly could have been. It seems reasonable to guess there could well be dozens of such sons of popes in those days.

Without comment, Dr. George continued, “Who was Caesar at this time and what year were you born?”

Considering that “Caesar” was changing every few years as a new soldier-emperor took over, this would be shaky data indeed. The doctor did not specify what he meant by “at this time.” We know it was the African emperor, when Strages was born, but the name Strages gave sounded like “Vartru” to the typist. *Varu,* the closest form in Latin, would mean “knock-kneed.” Lacking a picture of the emperor, we can’t tell whether Strages was making fun of him or just giving a name.

“What was the position of Christianity in the early years of your life—with reference to its acceptance?”

“It was not accepted,” Strages said, “except by us. We Romans had the ‘Aryans’ to fight with. The only way to get rid of them was to kill them all, and we did it, later on.”

“How did you do that?”

“We speared them. I was in one of the battles. There were lots of them.” He was matter-of-fact; this was his business. Could this possibly have been the same soul who hated and despised the Romans a century and a half earlier? It was the use of the spear by the Roman soldiers that had so horrified Achmesh.

Calling the enemy “Aryans” doubtless came from Al’s supply-side observer, but it covers the people in what we call the Indo-European family of languages, which was believed to have begun and spread from the Mesopotamian area northward and later to be misidentified by Hitler as a “pure race.” These people would not have been exposed to the Christian teachings unless by a few hardy travelers—until some years later (unless there were “undercover”

Christians among the units of the Roman army).

The Goths came down from northern Europe and the others from countries like Syria, Assyria, and Persia, with a taste for what they could pillage and plunder in the now-declining Roman Empire.

With his urge for history, Dr. George asked, "What was the name of the battle?"

"In the year 256, in the Mesopotamian plain—the battle of the plains. More than 400,000 people were killed, of the Aryans."

Was this possible? We know this soldier enjoyed bragging. But also, history books tell us there was hot fighting in the Mesopotamian area then. However, the closest battle to that date was a calamitous *defeat* for the Romans. But if Strages were to fudge the dates a bit (and who looked at calendars then anyway?), a few years later the Roman army did strike back and reduced the Syrian city of Palmyra to ruins. Since there were no war correspondents, just military messengers, and fewer people learning to read than formerly, anything the Roman soldier said about the battle would just have to be accepted.

The gist of his conversations with Dr. George indicated that Captain Slaughter was a pragmatic, insensitive soldier to whom killing was just a way to get things done.

Asked again if, in the battle of the plains, the Romans were victorious, the husky voice said, "Yes. Every man was killed on the field, including the general. It was the only way Christianity could win. Kill them all. All the nonbelievers."

This was none of the personalities they had seen before, certainly not the gentlemanly James or the young soldier, Jack Carstairs, horrified by the blood and guts of the battlefield. This was a man who used force, who took it for granted.

"Your general is a Christian?"

"Yes, he was Christian. He believed in the Holy Trinity.

These other people don't so we kill them all." It was as simple as that.

"Were you married?"

"Hardly anybody gets married" was the shrugging answer. "If you want to take some women, it's all right."

No comment from the doctor, but, "Did you have children?"

"Lots of them." As if they were objects, like toys.

Could this have been the same inner person who nearly wept speaking of the son he had lost in France?

"Did you have any affection for your children?"

"No, what for?" He seemed surprised at the question. "Christianity is the only thing now. Christianity must reign. Everything else is trampled under foot."

Protested the doctor, "That was not the teaching of Christianity, not bloodshed and violence."

"Muscarcareh," said the captain, "Muscarcareh." In Latin *muscaria* would mean "fly swatters," what you'd use on pesky insects, or *mus carcare* (close to the exact sound that Al spoke) would mean "in a mouse trap" or "trivial, trivial annoyances." The soldier continued, "What they taught me, that's all I know."

He confirmed that he was both a Roman soldier and a Christian—at least in the time frame where he was answering the questions. He was well received by his superiors. "I never see anything wrong; I did what I was told to do. I was a soldier." Right: the kind of soldier crooked politicians would prefer, it seems.

Asked if he was harsh with his slaves, he said, "No." This was normal. Romans who had money used slaves as we would hired help, but also knew they'd get far better work from them if the slaves had decent conditions. Slaves who committed crimes against their masters were something else. The greatest source of slaves was war captives, and a captain was in a good position to get some. A captain would be a fairly wealthy man at this time. In fact, the emperor Caracalla, who ruled from 211-217 A.D., increased the pay of the army so greatly it was "ruinous to Rome's declining economy."[5] Strages could probably afford one of the better homes and a supply of slaves.

The doctor continued, asking about the church. Was it corrupt? Strages confirmed that it was. "I found out when I was sixty years old that the church had control of the army, but I didn't know this before." It is possible that the Christians were now so intermingled with the general population and so full of the intensity of conversions that would make good soldiers that, without it being a matter of public knowledge, they did gain a great many army posts. Indeed, how else, in another fifty years, would Constantine have the nerve to openly pray for his army and then proclaim a Christian nation if he weren't certain of military Christian backing?

"Were there any great congresses or meetings of the church Fathers?" If Strages had been a bishop himself, he could have answered that.

"I spent most of my time in the army in the field. I didn't go to any."

"Do you as a Roman soldier believe in the resurrection?"

"Resurrection of what?

"Of the Christ."

"I don't understand it. There is only the doctrine of Father, Son, and Holy Ghost. Amen."

"What is the attitude of most of the Romans toward the story of Jesus?"

"Don't have any attitudes. Just mostly living for today. I don't know much about Christ."

Dr. George kept on asking about church organization and military matters, leaving out details of personal life. Captain Strages stayed in character, with his brief answers showing pride in the slaughter and the victories. He boasted of the campaign in Gaul where he claimed 100,000 people a year were killed, when he was a mere twenty-two years old.

After describing victories in Helvetia (Switzerland), he turned his head and said, "There's somebody . . . " then paused.

"Tell us who you see," said Dr. George. He sensed a shift in time and place. The observer knew the date and place:

"Blue eyes, the year 233, the place Venice. Someone is there, so beautiful, blue eyes, blonde hair. It is she whom you know as Gladys Davis, in 1952. The year 233; her name . . . Brunhilde. It is not a Roman name. She is Viking and has blonde hair and blue eyes."

"Is she of the Helvetian people? or of Gaul?"

"No, farther north, what you know now as Norway." The observer was keeping an eye on the past and present. "I *married* Brunhilde."

With this Viking, Captain Slaughter had married, unlike the women he had lived with earlier. She *was* different. She, he admitted, was a Christian.

"What was the religion of her people?"

"*They* believed the Norse gods ruled the winds. She became a Christian." It is probable that the blonde woman had been captured and brought by the far-ranging Roman military to Italy, where prisoners would fetch a high price as slaves. There is a story that the bishop of Rome, seeing such blonde captives paraded down the highway, had asked who they were; "Angles" (taken from among the Angles and Saxons of early Britain), the military man had replied. "No," the bishop replied—"They're not Angles, they are *angels*."

"And did she try to convert you to Christianity?"

He shrugged. "Wasn't interested . . . She did."

So that was why, after 233, he had followed the Christian belief—at least in name—without apparently altering the pragmatic fighting business.

"Did you have children by her?"

"One. One child, male."

"Does that personality carry over? Have you known him in any other incarnation?"

Said the observer, "I knew him in Egypt as Ra Ta."[6]

"In what time in Egypt was he known as Ra Ta?"

Then the observer said, "I knew him 20,250 B.C."[7] The earliest written records so far appear to be about 3,000 B.C. We know from the paintings and art of Thera, in the Mediterranean, that there probably was civilization far earlier than our records reach; we have seen the drawings on rocks found in the desert, and we have seen the drawings in the caves of Lescaux. But we have only radiocarbon dating to help place them in the terra time frame.

Regardless of timing, here is a relationship with the seer—and perhaps, by this time: July 10, 1952—Al had already learned enough about Edgar Cayce to know what some of his former incarnations had been. So it is possible that information was being used about the name Ra Ta from his conscious memory, but the date, 20,250 B.C., was 10,000 years earlier than the date given in the Cayce readings.

Could he tell more about his child with Brunhilde? Strages, who had no interest in his earlier offspring, certainly could talk about this one. His name was Paul. Yes, he was named after the apostle. "I named him," he added proudly.

This change in his attitude toward women and children, and even toward careers of others, came about after he had married the Viking woman. Before that, he showed no pride, no real interest in the children he had earlier.

Henry George asked, "Did he (Paul) become a soldier?"

"No. He was a builder. He went around, when he grew up, and taught people how to build. He had hundreds of people come to hear him. I did not see much of him."[8] Interesting that the captain bragged little about killing after speaking of his marriage to Brunhilde and the birth of his son, Paul.

There are possible connections here, which Paul the builder represents, with other parts of Al's lives: *building*—he had a part in Solomon's temple; Jesus was a carpenter and later had many people come to hear Him. And we recall that Achmesh's occupation was carpenter and builder—and Jack Carstairs had also worked at the trade. The name *Paul* was also that of the converted Saul, one whom Achmesh hated, but whom Strages would have considered historic.

The doctor never asked Strages about his childhood, perhaps because he had serious doubts about the factuality of the answers. Without background research, without a strong knowledge of the Latin language and of Roman history as well as the history of the Christian church, a person who contrasted the subject's answers only with popular perceptions of that time might have considered the answers as fabrications or fantasy.[9]

The Roman soldier, Captain Strages or Captain Slaughter, simply took life as a strong man would—took his pleasure with women (until he met Brunhilde) and his business with soldiering, killing people not because he was evil but because he was told to. He lacked the pleading and joy of Achmesh, he was at times grim and cynical. But he did find the Viking woman a force of change in his life. He seemed to care about only her as a wife and about only their child as his son.

The doctor drew out the information that Captain Strages had died in Ostia, a port of ancient Rome, in 280 A.D., at a ripe age for a Roman soldier—seventy-nine..

11

Greeks Bearing Gifts and Ships Bearing Cedars

July in Virginia Beach. One more session to go.

It was about to come true—the most wonderful thing Al could ever wish in *this* life: he and Gladys would be man and wife. Gladys's friend, Lydia J. Schrader-Gray, who had been one of the witnesses of the fourth session, had volunteered her home for the wedding. A small, intimate group gathered, and a few moments after midnight on July 20 they spoke the wedding vows. Al looked at Gladys with tears in his eyes. "Don't laugh," he whispered, "but I see angels." Nobody laughed.

They shared Gladys's little home, where the words, "Glad Niche," were inscribed on the front walk, near the shore of the gentle lake just three blocks from the ocean. Al would continue working at the firm in Philadelphia for the time being, spending weekends at the Beach until he could phase out his work "up north" and begin again at the Beach.

What he had not counted on were strange happenings—someone else might have called them "psychic gifts." "Gifts" like these he didn't need. They were worries he didn't understand, possibly psychic in origin. They might have been related to the strain of the seven-hour drive to Philadelphia on either side of the weekend, but it was more than that. Gladys tried not to say, "I told you so," but he knew how she felt.

It had happened three times in the past three weekends. When a couple of friends had stopped by and they had begun a friendly game of cards, Al looked so strange that Les asked him, "Did you see a ghost?"

Al nodded and made a face. "A ghost of your cards. I can see the cards you've got in your hands." Les held them close against his chest and Al proceeded to call them off.

"I'll be damned," Les slammed the deck down and left the table. "No contest if you know everything I've got."

Al sighed and laid his down. "Sorry. I don't know how it happened." There was some half-hearted kidding about how he could now make a killing at cards, if he could find anyone willing and dumb enough to play with him.

The friends talked a bit, then left. So much for the pinochle they had looked forward to.

The next incident was unexpected and embarrassing. Al was leaving the bus station platform when he noticed a woman in a plaid coat about to cross the street. He saw a dark figure lunge from the shadow and snatch her pocketbook—but then realized she still had it, and the shadow wasn't in sight. He stepped up and touched her elbow. He warned her to watch her pocketbook, but she pulled away angrily.

"Take your hands off me or I'll call a cop!"

He stepped back, embarrassed. In a few minutes he heard her scream. How had he known what was going to happen?

Later, their friend Bob had stopped by to visit with Al and

Gladys. Al "saw" something, as Bob was preparing to leave and warned, "Be careful on the way home. You might get a flat tire going over the bridge."

An hour later, Bob phoned. "Thanks a lot," he said with an edge in his voice. "You sure fixed me up with that flat tire—and in the rain, too." It did no good to protest. Somehow, Bob felt that Al was to blame for the misfortune. After all, he did predict it.

Al was frustrated. If he *had* to see the future, why couldn't he see happy things? Or if he saw unhappy ones, why couldn't he prevent them? This was an ability that brought no joy. "Do you think God wants to punish me for trying to see into the future," he wondered aloud, "letting me see future problems but not prevent them?"

Gladys reassured him that whatever was happening was probably something inadvertent that he had done without intending to. For he had certainly had nothing but good intentions. "Remember you told me about those times you studied to develop psychic power. Perhaps," she said, "now having all these sessions under hypnosis, you have opened up a center—somewhere inside you—and made it so sensitive it picks up certain things about to happen."

One thing Al knew, as he prepared for the eighth session, he was not going to have any more of the hypnosis. He was glad to know about the past, but he was going to thank God for the *present* and just do the best he could.

He recalled reading Greek myths at school, where he had learned about the Trojan princess, Cassandra. Apollo, the god of prophecy, had granted her the gift of foresight when he thought they'd be lovers. When she turned him down and went her own way, Apollo couldn't take back the gift of seeing the future—but he could fix it so she would never be believed. So when she cried out to warn the Trojans that the horse the Greeks had built was a danger to the city, they laughed at her—and the Greeks won. The entire kingdom of Troy had fallen because of Greeks bearing gifts. Too bad that had become such an axiom of suspicion. Al did not want to share Cassandra's fate.

When the final session did arrive, the evening of August 14, he made a point of asking Dr. George if he would be sure to take him to the life that seemed to hold so much innocent fun and companionship. He had felt so light-hearted each time he recalled being Longo's friend on the sunny Mediterranean shore.

Of course, if he could find a reason for having lives of tremendous contrast: the life of the Jew who saw Christ, the life of the Roman soldier for whom killing was just a business, and the life of the cold-numbed Siberian—if they could understand any kind of development behind that—*that* ought to help.

Dr. George agreed and, when he was in trance, told Al to go back and look for Longo. There was an almost immediate response:

"He has a black hat."

"Who has a black hat?"

"I don't know what he's doing; he's walking over the sand dunes, and he's got a black hat. Now, wait a minute, he's coming over and I'll ask him—Hey, Longo! Hey, Bongo! . . . He says he was riding a camel, and he found the hat while he was riding. He gave it to me, and look at it."

"What is it made of, this black hat?"

"Hemp. We get the hemp from the wachen tree. We make clothes out of it." (See note on bark cloth, p.79.) "He gave me the hat and I put it on. It feels awful good. Longo gives everybody everything. Wait a minute . . . Here he's coming with a whole bunch of us. There are seventy-four of us. He's going to teach us to sing. I wish I could sing like Longo." Suddenly he blurts, "Oh, my goodness, that's too loud, Longo! Aah." (Apparently the sound grew softer to the listener.)

"You can't see him now, can you? Sing that loud. It is called (a name that sounded like) Iclungtochua." After singing one tuneful group of syllables, the singer changed to the song they had heard the first time: "Aliman, nocha, nocha . . . "

"That's a very nice song," Dr. George said approvingly. "Will you translate it for us?"

Instead of giving the identical words from the first time, the singer offered different words but with a similar meaning: "The sky is beautiful. It's awful clear night tonight, there is a full moon."

Then Al paused and in a changed tone announced, "It is now October 21, 953 A.D. He wants to sing another song, 'Tranda tranda bong.' "

"What does that mean?"

In a prayerful tone, the singer explained, "In His infinite capacity the Lord most high taketh His little children thus nigh up in His arms and comforts us." He added, in a musical roar, "Traddilup. Bojum bojium, bojium traddilup tooo—tooo!" He appeared to converse with the songleader: "I like that, Longo. Let's sing that some more." He turned to the questioner: "Isn't he beautiful? He has the face of the Christ, in his infinite wisdom. Nobody knows as much as Longo." Finally, for the first time, he identifies himself: "My name is Wachwa Wachwa." He sings again, then listens. "Oh, Longo, where did you get that song? That's beautiful."

"And what does that song mean?" the careful doctor asked.

"Here within us lies infinite spirit. Give and it shall be given unto you. There are many stars out tonight, millions of them." It is the ecstasy that comes from contemplating infinity.

Always ready for more data, Dr. George breaks in, "Will you say for us in your tongue, 'There are many stars out tonight.' "

Al sings nine ringing rhythmic words which the typist couldn't catch. Then his observer joins in. "I wish everybody could see Longo. He's John Foster Dulles in this present incarnation. And Longo knows more because he emerged with infinite spirit; he knew God, knew who He was, talked to Him. He tried to teach me."

"I'm sure that you learned a great deal from Longo. Now you stay with Longo and rest. They were happy days with Longo."

Al breathed gently, relaxing. Then the doctor led him back to Achmesh, who saw Jesus sitting on a small donkey. The observer came in after Achmesh said he could not seem to get near Jesus, that something prevented him from getting close enough. Then Dr. George sought a detail:

"What prevents you from getting near enough to look at Jesus?"

"I don't know. There is a certain high rate of vibration. He said to Mary, 'Touch me not, for I am not yet ascended to my father that made me.' His vibrations are so high that if he had touched her it would have killed her."

That might sound strange but it parallels some studies and experiences of "higher beings." [Dr. James Fadiman, psychologist, spoke about "higher beings" in his address to the International Congress on Healing, June 23, 1993, noting that sometimes there is something so "high" that ordinary people cannot take it. "What you are seeing is what you *are capable of seeing*, not that which is actually manifest . . . so that you can handle it. And if you're in the Old Testament (they were instructed), 'Thou shalt not look upon the face of the Lord and live' . . . They say that yoga was designed to allow your body to be in decent enough shape so that when it dealt with energies that were higher than humans could usually handle, it would not burn out."]

Dr. George again wanted to look at the language: "Would you say that as he said it? In his native tongue?"

"Aramaic." Al spoke a series of words that ended, "Eloi, Eloi," then he appeared to see the mountain. "There is Mount Carmel. It's a big mountain, 452 feet high. Cedar trees grew on it, put by Solomon, cedars of Lebanon. I knew Solomon."

(Mount Carmel is big. But it's almost 1,800 feet high, four times the 452 feet the subject gave. It covers 95 square miles and has been called a sacred mountain since the fifteenth century B.C. The caves on its slopes are legendary. It is best known as the site of Elijah's victory over the prophets of Baal. And it *is* green with many nature areas and tall trees—including cedars of Lebanon, according to the *Britannica.* These cedars are in fact the wood used by Solomon to build his temple at Jerusalem. The Hebrew name for both tree and timber is *erez,* and the plural form, *arazim.* Interesting that *bulrushes* is a name that, in Hebrew, sounds almost like Achmesh—Acmeen. The Lebanon cedar grows, of course, on Mount Lebanon and on a few other higher mountains of Lebanon, Syria, and Turkey. It cannot survive in the warmer lowlands, which explains why Solomon bought his cedar timber from Hiram, king of Tyre, in exchange for wheat and oil. The logs were hauled to the sea and floated for 200 miles down the Mediterranean coast, then carried inland to Jerusalem.[1])

Dr. George did not miss his subject's last remark. He asked, "You knew Solomon?"

"Yes, I knew Solomon. Long ago. He brought those trees from Lebanon. I helped him put in those trees. He put them all on Mount Carmel."

The doctor had thought eight lives were plenty, and here was a ninth!

"Will you go back to the time of Solomon?"

The switch was quick this time because he had been thinking about it. "Ships we took them on, of Tyre." (It is interesting to note the non-English word order here. It follows more the classical pattern of speech.) As if proud of his success with the large assignments he was given, he gave the numbers: "We had forty-two ships, and in them we took a thousand trees. Just to put on Mt. Carmel. The cedar was also used for part of his temple."

Then he volunteered, "Solomon told me, in that period I was Onon, that there was a man going to be born who would save the world. He would become the Deliverer, the Christ." (*Christ* is "anointed one" from the Greek; the same meaning as *Messiah* or "Mashiah" in Hebrew; in Judaism the promised deliverer of the Jews.) He chuckled as he continued, "I told Solomon he didn't know what he was saying. I didn't think, with all his wisdom, that he could know this. I thought he was batty.

"Solomon said he's building the temple, and one day, he says, 'On, there will be a man who will come in this temple and his feats will be preserved for all time, the glory and tradition, and he will be the Christ.' " Then Onon added, "I seemed to be a doubter."

The doctor wanted to nail down some specifics: "What was your name when you were with Solomon?"

" On . . . On." He repeated it, as if the name might be Onon or even Onan.[2]

"Were you a worker in the temple?"

"No." He was far more important than that, it seemed. "Vice . . . What you call a vice consul." One who arranged for trading, products, commodities, even from other countries.

"But you saw Solomon, and you saw him work?"

"I saw Solomon, and I spent a great deal of time with Solomon. He's quite a man, but he had too much knowledge and it went to his head." A comment you might expect from one who felt quite sure of his own position.

Going for some financial details, the doctor asked, "Now tell me, what did Solomon pay his laborers?"

"Rolio. A rolio equals five shekels.[3] They got one a week."

"What was a rolio made of?"

"Gold."

"And what was a shekel made of?"

"Gold. A shekel was one fifth as big as a rolio."

"What was the symbol, what was on the face of the rolio?"

" On the face of a rolio, I see Solomon. I see a drawing of a man with a long beard."

"And on the face of a shekel?"

" You can find a lot of these in the inner temple, in the Great Pyramid of Giza." Here, the subject began to speak of the future: "When the temple is opened, lots of them will be found." He gave other details of the coins, describing the reverse side with words for "world" and "king." According to *Coins of the World*, R.A. G. Carson, Harper, 1962, they have found no coins further back than the fifth century B.C.

The vice-consul or commerce secretary began speaking as a wisecracking politician, a bit contemptuous of the leaders. "When I saw Solomon, he got so much wisdom he lost his head and just went cuckoo. He's a funny fellow; there are a lot of funny things I remember." His mood shifted and he recalled, "One trip to Lebanon . . . the smell of those cedar trees was sweet! We were lost in the Mediterranean Sea, we went up to Cyprus and there was a storm—I don't want to talk about that."

This was apparently where Solomon's vice consul or commerce secretary had died: in a storm at sea, near Cyprus. (This would make three deaths in the water, for this personality, if we do not count Gregor's death in the glacier.)

Onon the trading manager seemed well aware of money—even money not listed in any of the coin references checked—and had no hesitancy in mocking the king. Either he was speaking from a view apart, as an observer, or he was both unafraid and disrespectful. Perhaps both. The experience of this identity seemed to be one of superficial values. As the observer, he could realize by seeing the future that he was wrong.

But was there really a point to this? A pattern that made sense out of a mix of lives?

Because this was Al's final session, Dr. George wanted another interview with Achmesh. When he suggested that, his subject sounded a bit worried.

"I seem to get all tangled up in that storm all the time."

"You may leave that storm," said the doctor, ready to move on.

"I don't want to leave it. I don't want to leave it!" (There was emotional contradiction there. The doctor was willing to see what would happen.)

"Then you stay there and tell us what you see."

" 'Get away from me, you filthy people!' They push me down. Why can't they get along? It's cold, it's lightning. 'Let me go!' (Agitation was evident.) 'Crucify him, crucify him!' somebody is saying. Can't you see him?"

"Will you say that in your native tongue?"

"Crux, Crux, Crux, Tagge!" the typist wrote. Of course, we know *crux* is *cross* in Latin. *Tagge* could be the rapid Latin pronunciation of "Tu age"—a = ah, g = as in go, e = eh—which would translate as "The cross! The cross! The cross! Go do it!" Al did not know Latin, but doubtless in the crowd Achmesh heard Romans yelling as well as Jews. This was certainly Roman talk.

Achmesh felt compelled to speak again of the man on the cross, but now in a different way: "He's bleeding! It's that man, Jesus, again. The farther I go I seem to find that man Jesus. It is cold, April 2, 33 A.D. Golgotha. There's a man there. He's a good man, but they crucify him. His blood is coming out of his right eye. Some winds are blowing his hair back and forth. He is a strong man, a big , strong man.

" 'Mother, behold thy son,' he says to a woman. Where did she come from? All those other people went away, and it's awful cold. 'Father, it is into thy hands I commend my spirit.' A man came. Here he is taking him down from the cross, pulling the nails out. (He describes their length and placement.) He's taking him away. (He describes solid oak boards and poles they set the body on.) He's still bleeding. I can get up close now and see his face; his eyes are open. He's looking at death with a heavenly smile. (He speaks to the other man.) What are you doing here, Nicodemus? (Nicodemus has come with a friend. Al describes how the two men carry the body a distance and up a mountain path, higher and higher to a door to a cave.) They take Jesus into the cave, and the cave is all dark. I'm going in. Now it is all light. Isn't that funny? All dark from outside, but when you get inside, it has the brilliance of a noonday sun. He lights it up, Jesus does, the light is from him. He said, 'I am the light,' I remember that now."[4]

Dr. George continued asking Achmesh to repeat words in Aramaic. When he asked for something that was said in the cave, the subject answered, "It is not to be given at this time."

Soon, however, the observer had shifted to an earlier time and said:

"Twenty-nine A.D. July 1st again."

A chance for more data. "What is July 1st in your calendar or in the Roman calendar?"

"Ooley," the typist wrote. (She spelled it another time, "Euly.")

Dr. George persisted, "And as the Romans would call it?" He did not realize that the subject had done *exactly* that. The month of July, to the Romans, would be *mensis Juli* (or month of Julius, as they named it for Julius Caesar), and the proper Latin pronunciation of *Juli* would be "Yooley," just what Al had been trying to say. But because his hypnotist asked again, the subject apologized, "I don't know any other language in this body." Then he continued with his story, as he observed it.

"Twenty-nine A.D.; 4,125 people. I counted them: 4,125

people, and there is Jesus. He's talking to these people and they are seated all over a mountain and his voice carries, clarion clear."

"And what does he say?"

" 'That which I am, I was, and am now. If you will, children, ye may approach divinity and become divine. Come to me, little children, and let me show you the pathway to the Father. That's all there is. He came here and I brought you, as Amilius.[5] I brought you here. I want you to come back to the Father with me. Don't you want to come back, little children? For there is in the heavens the glory in the thirty-second plane of consciousness, the glory that only comes through service. If ye will, little children, come with me in service, in service to thy brother.' "

Achmesh appeared to enjoy describing the scene: "Some fellow got up, and he's a tough guy and he said, 'Who's my brother?' and Jesus said, 'Whatsoever a man follows, he loves. Love is, was, and will be. You are all part of my kingdom.' And the tough guy got up again, he's a Roman soldier, and he said, 'Who's my neighbor?' "

Instead of waiting for the answer, Dr. George interrupted and asked, "What language does he say that in?"

"Aramaic." In that case, the Roman would have picked up the local tongue, probably a helpful skill if he wanted to make friends among the ordinary people.

Achmesh spoke some words. The typist wrote, "Ardeltwine tod ardeltwine too." Then he explained, "It does not make sense to you, but then Jesus looked at him with such compassion and said to him, '*You* are my neighbor.' The Roman sat down."

Achmesh continued, as if this had been bottled up inside him and there was much more to come out. "Jesus said, 'I came that you might have life and more abundantly, and even as Isaiah said, "The wilderness shall be filled with roses and the lame shall leap and the blind see." I came that ye might see that you will be mine, and all things mine are thine, that the Father has sent me.' " He talked for over an hour.

This emotional outpouring was filled with Bible verses possibly from Al's subconscious memory, but given with rephrasing of the meaning rather than the exact words of the King James Version of the Bible with which Al was most familiar. At the end of the hour, the doctor asked, "Do you wish to tell us more about Achmesh?"

"Not now." There was a feeling of contentment.

"You will rest then," Dr. George said, but followed that with, "I would like to have you visit your people in Siberia once more, in the year 820. I would like to have you greet us in your native tongue."

"The town, Yakut," Al answered. Doubtless he thought the word was "town" instead of "tongue." The town was "450 miles from Vladivostok. Ice, ice, ice all over. Dandiwach. Handiwach."

"What does *Dandiwach* mean?"

"'Hello.' My name is Gregor; 825 A.D. Father's name is Gregorovitch."

"What does Gregor mean?"

"The world." (Actually, one meaning is "watchman." The other is "wakened, raised, raised from the dead.") The observer is commenting as fatigue must be settling in: "Simple name doesn't make any sense. This place full of ice doesn't seem to make any sense. Oh, cold. It's 42 below zero. I've got one coat made of rabbits. There are a lot of rabbits around here. Goodness gracious. We eat them up and make coats out of them." (Rabbits were probably easier to catch and eat than the snow leopard he mentioned the first time.)

"And where do you live?"

"In Yakut, underground."

"Why do you live underground?"

"It's too cold above ground. Ice."

"What are your words for 'It's too cold'?"

"The language of Yakut is peculiar. Only 450 people in this town. 'It's too cold' is (the typist writes): Onecingdown. It is always too cold.

" 'What are you doing here, Gregor?' somebody asks me."

Then Gregor speaks with this other entity, who explains there is a reason for his suffering. Jesus had shown the way, Jesus had suffered for others. Told that he had to work out his karma, Gregor died—but the subject added, with some satisfaction, that it was "good riddance of that body. It was tough."

"And now you will rest, you will rest, you will rest."

Here, the final suffering of this body meant the opening of "God's other door," as death was called by Edgar Cayce.

For Gregor and for the other lives, death is not an ending, but a transition.

12
The Master and the Man

Dr. George had prepared these questions carefully. The evening of July 15, 1952, was the next to the last of the hypnotic sessions with Albert Turner, and it was time to ask for the theme or motif of these different lives. Dr. George himself was not so concerned about themes as he was about verifiable evidence of the past lives, but Al was quite concerned; he wanted and needed to find a pattern and direction.

The man in the trance was breathing regularly.

The hypnotist led him first through the life that interested him and the witnesses the most, the life of the Hebrew, Achmesh, then through that of the Roman soldier, and finally through the chill Siberian life of Gregor. This was the time:

"Now I'm going to ask you if it is possible for you to look back on these three experiences—as Achmesh, as the Roman, and as this man from the North. And can you give us the master motif of your lives?

"Can you see a connection, a reason, a purpose for your having come into each of these forms and times and peoples?

"What was the lesson you had to learn? Why were you given the opportunity of living—again and again?"

That should do it. The questions were addressed not to any *one* of those individuals, but to someone who could answer for *all* three. Would this someone be able to give an understandable version of what was happening with the forces of the inner life?

The one who came through spoke slowly, like a patient teacher trying to make the problem clear to someone whose understanding was slower, like a master authority dealing with a pupil who had not quite grasped the concept.

"Each experience was given that this soul might cease to go further from God and draw closer. Experiences taught this soul less dependence on self. The experiences taught this soul that it must have many more experiences to learn to depend less completely on self.

"In these three experiences, the soul entered three bodies; the body tried to dictate to the soul, to have the soul's complete dependence on the body, and the kingdoms of the body having dominion over all things.

"The experiences given were to teach the soul to rely *not* on the house of the body, but to rely completely on the universe. To progress out of the body through those experiences that might be necessary to cloak that soul in a better body . . .

" . . . so that the body may not be dominant, and may use those experiences as lessons in teaching: that the soul is making its way back. And that *the body should help and not dictate.*

"That is the lesson taught this soul."

The witnesses looked at each other. Who was this speaking? The voice was not familiar to them, the tone was not that of the chilled cave dweller huddled in rabbit fur. Nor was it Achmesh, sometimes hesitant, sometimes frightened, sometimes boldly emotional. Neither was it the rough-and-ready soldier. Could it be the same kind of being who had spoken to Edgar Cayce in his trances? Dr. George, who had heard Edgar Cayce speak, didn't think so. But it had to be a master.

The message was not complex, it was clear and simple. Deceptively simple. Like "Love one another." *That* would have as many variations as there are people, multiplied by that same number to include all the possible relationships! It would have been more literary, more eloquent perhaps, to have something that went on for many paragraphs of rich prose, filled with esoteric words. But literary eloquence would not have had this impact.

Whatever being was speaking, each sentence, though in simple words, was loaded with meaning.

—First, the soul was in the body, the soul and body were able to affect one another, and the soul was not drawing as close to God as it should.

—Second, those incarnations were to teach the soul that by itself it would not get very far. It was still in early stages of the soul-body relationship. It would need more experiences to learn that the body was here to help the soul progress, not vice versa. It would need to *learn.* Literally learn from experience.

—Third, the hardest part to accept was that the soul should "rely completely on the universe"—when the universe seemed so vast, so impersonal! And yet this was saying that the universe was God or a part of God—and implying that there was a Universal Consciousness. Some great thinkers and scientists today are just daring to speak about this concept[1] . . . a nearly impossible idea for most of us.

—Finally, so that the body may not be dominant and may use these experiences as lessons; that the soul is trying to learn as it is making its way back.

Was this a variation of Jung's view of an attempt to understand the human psyche by approaching it from the outer or physical world? Neither the witnesses nor the man in trance realized how dramatically the body-soul relationship was to be demonstrated later.

Most of this reflection came to Al after the session was over, after he spent some time recalling the Master's message. It would come to him sometimes like a troubled dream—how the physical, the body, had dictated his reactions. As Achmesh, he had felt physical distress and disgust at the actions of the Romans and those of the crucifiers; as Strages, he had used physical violence instead of reason, in following military directions, and physical pleasure was his thought with the women he first had. As Peter/Gregor, he was aware of a frighteningly cold physical world, the strong forces of nature in Siberia. And he had separated from his tribe, from the others. That was when he had died in the ice.

While they had this being, this master, "on the line" as it were, Dr. George thought they might learn more—perhaps about a present identity of some soul who was one of those that Al had encountered on his time trek. But meanwhile, since the subject seemed to be uncomfortable, the hypnotist wanted to move him to a more pleasant era. He could move him to the warm Mediterranean shore, and then see if the master would talk about someone or something else.

By far the sunniest in personality was that black singer in Tripoli, whose leader led his tribe in song to honor the Maker of the sun and stars and moon. Even though he spoke of no "religion" as such, his songs seemed filled with harmony and appreciation for the infinite, for nature and the sky (in essence, the universe!).

"And then you went into the body of a Negro in Tripoli and you knew Longo," Dr. George reminded his subject. "Had you known him before?"

Because he addressed his question to the Tripolitan, it was not the master but the black man who responded: "He was a great man, a kind, a just man." However, it seems the observer was waiting in the wings to help, as the doctor continued and asked, "Who was Longo?"

"In a previous experience, Longo was St. Paul. Longo now is John Foster Dulles." The subject spoke confidently. "Longo has all knowledge, he knows where the stars came from, he tries to teach us." This lyrical answer was typical of the Tripolitan life, but of no other. He continued as he had before, in almost a sing-song voice. "He used to spend day after day, to teach us all, as we sat there in a circle. He taught us to sing, to love God who *was* the stars and the moon. He told us why the stars were up there, to make us better and stronger. He taught us that the moon was our mother. He divided up our wages each night. He told us that the sun made the earth retain the heat so that we would be warm at night after the sun left. He taught us everything. He was all-wise father, Longo was. Most of all, he taught us to sing."

After this paean of praise, the Tripolitan fell silent. The master did not speak again.

Dr. George thanked Al for his cooperation. They promised to keep in touch.

The group said their good-bys and left. In the coming months, the researcher-physician would continue to assemble his data on the people who recalled past existences. The witnesses, members of the Theosophical Society, would get on with their lives.

As Al prepared to leave, he was asking himself: Is this really the end? It somehow seemed as if time did not really exist. How could it exist if people could move back and forth from one life to another? Was it human memory they were dealing with here, or was it something else? How could they tell? It was too much for him at the moment. If he meditated, it would come.

Heading home, he welcomed the solitary night. His heart was beating rapidly, but his spirit was remembering the words of the master guide; especially, "The soul is making its way back."

He recalled the last words of the Siberian: "Jesus showed us the way, and you've got to do it, too. You've got to suffer . . . It was a good riddance of that body. It was tough."

A wry thought: There had been *no* life of his without suffering, unless the black singer—but he remembered with painful clarity that the singer had started as the son of a slave who had been beaten to death. So there was no exception; all of the lives had some.

He recalled the last moments of Achmesh, who had finally given himself wholly to the high ecstasy crying, "Glory, glory!" He *had* given his body to the cause, hadn't he? At the end, in any case? Yes, Achmesh had been rather timid, uncertain, had tried to hear the great Teacher but hadn't really been able to understand—yet he had ended caught up in the Christian fervor.

Why, then, had he come next as a Roman soldier, a callous man for whom killing was just a business? Why had he come back as the kind of man he had despised, had mocked, had actively hated in the previous life?

Of course, since he had led the soldier's life, had felt his feelings and was able to remember them, he admitted the soldier had a totally different outlook. The soldier depended greatly on the body—he kept safe with the sword. Enemies could do the worrying. A captain could live comfortably, be entitled to some of the rewards of the different battles. It was O.K. to play around with women; in fact, for some men it was expected. So, if children came along, well, that was the mother's concern. As the soldier, he didn't need to worry about them.

Strange how his attitude had shifted after he found that blonde Viking woman. After he married her, he had learned that a woman could be a strong character, not just for pleasure. He had even stopped fooling around. He wondered somehow why he had married her when he could have the other women for nothing. And then their child was born. Paul. A beautiful name. He had picked it. But where was the logic?

Why then should he have found himself next in the cold, bare necessities of the grim life as Gregor?

"Depend less on the body," the voice had said. The body hadn't done Gregor much good at all. But it *had* taken all of his energy just to keep it alive, with a cave for shelter, animal skins for clothing, and a wife—perhaps for extra warmth; they'd had no children.

Why?

Each of those lives had to be part of his soul picture, but he couldn't yet see where they fit. Recalling, seeing the different lives in his mind, reminded him of one of these labyrinth mazes where you try to draw your way to the center or, if you aren't careful, you end up in a blind alley—stuck, no progress. Or perhaps the different parts of the lives might seem like those scattered dots that make no sense at all on the page of the puzzle magazine—until you start connecting them, number one to number two, number thirteen to number fourteen, etc.—and once you make the proper connections, *there is the picture.*

13

Revealing Past Patterns

Light in the Karmic Catacombs

It should have been idyllic, the married life Al and Gladys began in the little cottage surrounded by fragrant camellias and gardenia bushes, complete with its own vine and fig tree.[1]

But there were two problems, more than just flies in the ointment; two shadows hanging over the sunny home. One was the strain of Al's weekly commuting to Philadelphia to Auchincloss, Parker, and Redpath. A seven-hour drive on each end of a weekend would be exhausting even if he hadn't had four previous heart attacks, and the five days in between were lonely. But he and Gladys were convinced this was the right track. There could be no change of home or job for Gladys; she continued as secretary of the A.R.E., continued her work indexing the readings and working with the Cayce materials. Al did survive the commuting, gradually phasing out the Philadelphia activities, and by the end of 1952 had a little office behind the garage of Glad Niche.

The second shadow was the additional intrusion of disturbing flashes into Al's consciousness at odd and unexpected moments, troubling bits of precognition, where he foresaw accidents but couldn't prevent them. There was the time the auburn-haired matron came down the post office steps. Urgently he told her, "Excuse me, Miss. Please don't get in that car!"

She was startled, indignant. She snapped, "What's wrong with you? You crazy or something?" as she opened the door of her friend's car. Al felt as if *he* had been struck when he heard the crash two minutes later.

He was upset as he told Gladys about the incidents. "When are these things going to stop?" he asked miserably. "It's not right that I should be getting them when I can't use them to help anybody!"

Gently Gladys reminded him of Edgar Cayce's advice that developing a spiritual relationship should come *before* stressing psychic skills. Of course, Al was working on that now. These manifestations could be side effects, she surmised, from the earlier psychic exercises he had worked on, and they would probably fade. (They did, within three years.)

Now Al had the memories of his nine lives—and no longer needed any proof that he had lived before. He had originally gone looking for the past, wondering if it was there, hoping he could find it. Now he knew it was there, knew he had lived those lives. And he knew he had to learn from it—it was even more important than a matter of life and death. It was a matter of life *and what came after life.* Whatever it was, it was not "death."

But just having the memories and not doing anything about it would be like sitting in a restaurant and just looking at the food.

What did they really have to work with?

He and Dr. George were looking for different things. Henry George had accepted him as a volunteer to see what could be discovered with solid identification of characters and data that would be proof of historical-quality past lives. What Al had spoken from his subconscious or his inner memory of his past selves, for the most part, was now on the transcripts his typist had made of the sessions. Though Dr. George never said so, in some of the lives his manner—for example in questioning "James II"— indicated he considered this character as so much fantasy. By the way the physician avoided coming back to a life—such as "James's," for example, or an odd remark between lives—Henry George eliminated them from further discussions.

Today those who collect accounts of past lives with verifiable information are amassing plenty of data. It would please Dr. George to know that a great many accounts of precise recollections of past lives are already available, from Dr. Ian Stevenson's closely documented stories like that of Shanti Devi, to Dr. Weatherhead's accounts, such as Captain Battista's little daughter, to the amazing recent story on *Unsolved Mysteries* of the young man from New Jersey who not only recalled a life as a South Carolina youth who died in a submarine accident—but also met and identified his family. Today's therapists do not believe, as the early ones seemed to, that they have to convince the public and begin at square one. They are not so devoted to pinning down times, dates, and places in the past as they are to *using* the information to help free their clients from pains of the past. They are looking for *uses* of the knowledge of past lives, rather than simply their existence.

Fortunately, with Gladys's help, Al managed to solve enough of the cosmic puzzle to unlock new areas of happiness and faith.

He was wondering how to go about it. There was so much

to remember if he was going to make sense out of it and do better in the present.

He pondered the different kinds of reality he had experienced. Plenty of the physical. Al had *felt* the wind and dirt on his face on the hill; he had *felt* the warmth in Tripoli, the numbing cold in Siberia. He had felt the pain of his battle wound, felt the alcohol that was poured over it. Whatever Dr. George thought about the truth of it, Al had been through *real* sensations, real emotions. Whether or not they proved to be recorded historically, they had been solidly, totally real inside him. Real and more valuable than dollars and cents for his own perspective on life. All he needed to do was trace the connections. To discover the elements. To find some kind of order in the patterns. To go from revealing to healing.

This, of course, is what a regression therapist helps a client do. Some professionals who have regressed several hundred clients, including Dr. Brian Weiss and Dr. Roger Woolger, believe that the factual occurrence of the experience in historic time is not the most important factor; it is the reality felt by the experiencer that makes a difference in his or her life.

Al would begin with an overview of each of the nine lifetimes, looking to see whether any elements were part of the present. Then he would see what elements—money, fighting, worship, skills, etc.—appeared in more than one life. Then see if there were connections in a pattern. If so, he would try to use that pattern to improve the present and his spiritual journey.

What was revealed in these lifetimes?

We know that there were nine different sets of mannerisms, there were even more than nine ways of speaking, nine sets of skills, fears, hopes, and loves. The recordings had revealed different personalities; the speech as Jack, for instance, was different in timbre and tone from that of

Gregor or Wachwa. Arrogance showed in the soldier, courtesy in James. Nine different individuals.

A stack of encyclopedias and other references did not identify any of these men as historical personages—but did make it evident each one *could have been there* in the place and time he said he was. For instance, the records in Columbus, Ohio, identified a Samuel Carstairs, the name of Jack's father, in the proper time and place—and the only Carstairs listed on that page.

We can begin the overview with the earliest life, Onon: The man who claimed to handle trade for Solomon discussed bringing cedar trees for the temple. He admitted that he thought the idea of an anointed Deliverer for the Jews was ludicrous. Onon died in the water, in a shipwreck. Was there a connection for Al's present? *Trading* was his occupation with the brokerage firm. Not in cedars, but still, he was trading in commodities. Al probably had made some wrong guesses, spiritually, as Onon did.

Probably there were other lifetimes between Onon in the 900s B.C. and Achmesh in the first sixty years A.D. But there is no way for us to learn, at this point.

Achmesh's trade was stonemason and carpenter. He saw Jesus, he hated Roman soldiers, he wanted to understand what was happening. He admired his rabbi, he listened to Jesus, and was horrified by the occurrences at the crucifixion—wanted to pass on Jesus' message, even if he didn't understand it all. In the present, Al wanted to understand, wanted to pass on the message. Achmesh swam across the Sea of Galilee to get closer to Jesus. In the present Al taught swimming safety for the Red Cross.

The seventh, Strages: The Roman soldier who admitted he was illegitimate, who enjoyed using women until he met the strong Christian woman he married; he believed what he was told to believe about religion and killed when he was told to kill. Just following orders, he showed little insight on right or wrong. But he was proud of his son, Paul, a leader and builder. Three elements seemed to repeat in the present: (1) Al enlisted in military service (but only for a brief period); (2) he had a "Paul" he admired, but a brother, not a son; and (3) Al's second wife was a strong Christian woman—Gladys, he said in trance, was then Brunhilde.

The sixth, Gregor: The Siberian struggled as a hunter to survive. He was safe when living in an underground cave with his tribe, but met death when he left his tribe and got lost on a glacier. He had a revelation at death. Al left his "tribe" to hitchhike across the U.S. in his teens. He had a struggle to survive but it was economic, not physical.

The fifth: The singer, Wachwa, covered up childhood misery with later group affection, songs, swimming, and easy living, with reverence for the leader and for nature as God. "No use for women." In his present life, from the time of his early twenties, Al did a lot of piano playing and singing. Swimming was also a part of past and present here—in fact, Wachwa died while swimming.

The fourth: The priest lived a mostly solitary life in Italy after the major plagues, observing rituals, praying, not discussing any rites, but watching an artist at work. A connection with the present was the ability to meditate in solitude and the study of Scripture. Al did watch his artist sister, Ruth, at work.

The third: James belonged to the royal court but ran off to France. He fell in love, fathered a child, had to be brought home. He felt guilt, tried to make up for it with later work for translators. In the present life, Al's hitchhiking was a form of running off. Courtesy and politeness, trying to avoid pain to others, was both past and present.

The second: Pierre had a short life with papa; then, as he died of drowning, a vision of Jesus. Al adored his papa and nearly died in an accident at age seven, when he, like Pierre, had a vision.

The first: Jack Carstairs was the first life with a remembered pleasant childhood, with loving parents. As a restless teen, he enlisted in the Union army. Wounded, he was sent home. He married a Chinese girl. He spent time between Philadelphia and Toronto, had a son who lived, a daughter who died at birth. He sold some horses, taught swimming, worked as a carpenter and in a mill. He played the drum in the army, the piano at home. He also visited a girl friend. He studied the Bible, tried to learn about God. He died of pneumonia. This time we can see many connections with his present life, including his daughter dying right after birth, a brief military stint, seeking God.

Many of the places, times, and circumstances he recalled—which did not seem to be historically possible on the surface—turned out to be not only possible but highly probable, after research. A small alteration in his account of James, for instance: considering him an illegitimate son rather than the actual James II (which he could not have been if his father was James I) would make the rest of his account fit the period.

Al had no therapist but Gladys as his guide, yet he was sure that he would find in these life patterns the signposts, at least, to peace. While doing his other work, he would also work on studying the patterns in his lives. If he could find the patterns, Al believed the healing could begin.

But an ominous thought came like a barrier.

In looking back on those nine past lives, was it love that let him suffer, even be crucified, as Achmesh? Love that let him kill, as the Roman captain? Love that let him freeze to death, as the Siberian? Have his leg bitten off, as the Tripolitan? Drown, as little Pierre? Love . . . what sort of love was that?

Then he seemed to hear a voice: "Love does not compel. Love leaves you free—to return the love or to leave it. Love is there for you—but it won't force you." Was that all in his head? Wherever it came from, it moved him close to tears as he began to understand.

In those lives and in this one, he made choices. If he made the wrong choice, the love would not send him to hell. It would set him in another life to relearn, as he had relearned about women. It hurt inside as he looked over the way he saw women in his lives.

As the Roman soldier, he had used and, in a sense, abused women by just enjoying several and then discarding them. Then he met Brunhilde and began a change in his attitude. In the next life as Gregor, he had married one woman, Pubichet, and treated her as a wife should be treated—but no children. It was painful to see, in his next life, how the powerful woman beat his father to death. He wondered, if he hadn't been kind to Brunhilde and Pubichet, would *he* have been beaten to death? He again learned something, after being in Longo's tribe without women, learned to accept and honor a woman because she was Longo's. Then, as if to stabilize his character toward women, he had the friar's life with *no* women. Then an opportunity to run away from his home, as "James Fitzroy," and find a sweetheart in France. He went ahead, she bore his son, then he was dragged back to England, and his loved ones went to convents.

He felt the lump in his throat, as he saw what he had done versus what he should have done. Finally, as Jack, he found and married a loving woman. He didn't treat her as well as he could have, but they did better than any of his other times; this was his *first* lifetime with a long marriage, a child, and a spiritual search for God.

His lives had been teaching periods! Yes, he *had* suffered. There could be a hell on earth—but there could be heavenly love as well.

He was developing a new kind of faith. It *was* love that had let him be crucified as Achmesh—because that love knew he was going to live again with a better spirit.

A question of philosophy: Would it do anything for God if he loved God back? What value would human love be to God, he puzzled, if God could just manufacture bundles of it and give them back to Himself? If He could work people like puppets, so they would always bow down and worship? Al felt a stronger glow as he neared an understanding. It was *because* these souls were *free to choose* that when they chose Love, Light, and Life, their choices would increase the joy in the Divine. So having humans like him *free to choose* made their love for God more valued.

It was beginning to reveal a connection, a purpose for all the experiences.

He prayed—between times and at the beginning and end of each day as well. He felt as if God were telling him, "Seek Me, daily."

He knew he was loved now; he had Gladys and dear friends as well. Now to put things in order. Not too difficult, looking at the number of parallel points in his past experiences.

Dr. Roger J. Woolger, in his informative study, *Other Lives, Other Selves,* notes that there are often parallel points, parallel complexes, and parallel crises in present and past lives.[2] Al, slowly and sometimes painfully, began to see them and gradually experience the release and the accompanying healing.

He would continue to pray, to seek God in that way, but that was it. He would just live the best he could. Thinking of the future, yes, but accepting the fact that he could not control it. Realizing that what he *could* control was himself: his thoughts and his actions in the present. He felt a new sense of God's love, the feeling that everything would eventually fit into place.

ELEMENTS OF PAST LIVES EXAMINED

Reviewing the elements and problems of his past lives, he saw how they had been crisis points in this one, crises already surmounted, one way or another. He knew he was making some progress.

ELEMENTS

- The handling of money, of business activities
- The place of fighting, of the military, of killing
- Women, his relationship with them, with family
- The meaning and feeling toward a child, his child
- Religion, belief in God, in an afterlife; worship

After a long look at each one, he decided what was best to do in the present:

MONEY: Onon, Solomon's "Secretary of Commerce," had been sure of himself, cynical, commercial, ridiculing concerns about anything except successful trading, quality imports, healthy profits, and pleasant political power. Now he saw he had never been prosperous in any of his following lives.

Subsistence, yes, enough to get by on, but no successful business connection or high income. When he was the son of James I, when there was enough money for what he wanted to do, he did not have control over it. He had been oblivious to money as Achmesh, though comfortable as the Roman soldier, barely surviving as Gregor, living off the land as Wachwa the singer with only what surrounding sands and seas and plants supplied. He had been an austere priest with few if any amenities, in Italy; as Pierre, he drowned in an accident before he could tell what money meant. As Jack, he had worked as a carpenter for his father, and in Toronto he had worked in a mill, where he had an accident with a saw. As Al Turner, he never had enough money for really comfortable living, far from enough to satisfy his first wife, and though he was working with investments when he met Gladys, he never was what anyone would call "well off." Considering this element, he knew he would continue doing his best to work, but size of income would never be the main goal.

FIGHTING: As Achmesh, Al positively hated the Roman soldiers, despised and insulted them. (His crucifixion, however, was not from the Romans but from the Jews.) He was horrified by the sight of blood, whether from a spear wound, from a sword, or from the stones that "mashed" Stephen.

As the Roman soldier, he considered fighting as just a business. No visible reaction to woundings and killings. A completely opposite perspective. Then, as the friend of Longo, he seems to have no desire to use any weapons: "We don't believe in enemies." He stayed out of fights until the life of Jack Carstairs, when he thought he ought to enlist in the Union army. He was a man of peace as the friar.

In his present life, he had enlisted in the marines—but he got out as soon as he could. After seeing the elements of these lives, he knew he believed in peace even more. He became a Quaker, a member of the Society of Friends, who are well known for their pacifist stance. This fit the pattern that developed through his other lives; he was quite happy as a Friend. In fact, alongside the Virginia Beach Friends Meetinghouse are several gardenia bushes he planted.

WOMEN: The pattern of his relationships with women—as wives, sisters, mothers, or lovers—reached the extremes. The first life with any mention of women was that of the Hebrew, Achmesh; as a child, he had loved his mama, had been afraid when the strange man came to talk to him; he wanted his mama to comfort him. He also had an older sister who had been, as they say, sleeping around—at least she had been the wife of four of the men she'd slept with. Yet as Strages, *he* had been the one to play around—until he met the Viking woman, who "made him" become a Christian. Together they'd had a son who made them proud.

As Gregor, he said in answer to a direct question, he had a wife, but that was it. (Gregor's was a most important experience, however, as he—probably with a master's help—realized there was a purpose to his suffering.)

As the singer, he was as far from a glacier as one could get—on tropical sand under a tropical sun and *without any women*. Here, he had no use for women. He had an antipathy toward them. A royal princess beat his father, a black slave, to death. Women meant power and cruelty then. After he and other boys escaped their masters to live miles away with Longo, there was a bitterness under the surface joy, but a bitterness that rarely came to light. Only accidentally, as when Dr. George had asked, "Did you have a family?"

He had replied, "No. Then I wouldn't be happy! I didn't have anything, just me." He had convinced himself that a family meant unhappiness. "No use for women. We're happy." Would this hatred of a woman's lashing have contributed to the pattern that he did not have a family after this for nearly a thousand years! A therapist might have taken him back to see whether this woman was behind his subsequent problems, for there were troubles with women in *every* following life—except for the priest, who had no place in his life for them, and the little Pierre, who was too young for such things. With such a past-life pattern, he could have brought to this life a subconscious feeling that women were a source of unhappiness—until he met the one woman who had been a symbol of strength, had converted him, as the Roman. To Al, Gladys was the closest being to heaven.

CHILDREN: We catch glimpses of childhood experiences of this soul, first as Achmesh at age seven, seeking his mama in their tent (and later saying he can't recall any happy memories of that childhood). We get only a bitter feeling about Strages's childhood; he even brags about being illegitimate, never knowing or seeing his father. We don't know Gregor's childhood, but we do know that the Tripolitan's childhood held slavery and tragedy, though his adult life was happy. We know nothing of the friar as a boy, nothing of "James" as a youngster (though "James" fled to France at age fifteen and Al hitchhiked cross-country at seventeen; Pierre knew his father, but then came his drowning death and a vision. Jack Carstairs did have a happy childhood, a loving father and mother. This showed true progress in his personal family. It was very similar in his family this time.

What about *having* children? There was no indication he had even thought of any, until the Roman Strages, who had several by several women—then he met the blonde Viking, Brunhilde, and became monogamous and the father of Paul (named after the apostle)—Paul, who became a great builder and speaker. Could this have been an echo of Al's love for his next-older brother, Paul Flagler Turner? This beloved brother had been adored and admired by Al as much as the Tripolitan had admired Longo—who, he'd said, used to be St. Paul! (John Foster Dulles, identified as an incarnation of the admired Longo, was an outstanding Secretary of State under Dwight D. Eisenhower and an architect of U.S. foreign policy until his death in 1959.) Paul, Al's brother, was a student "Liberty Bond" salesman in World War I and an excellent speaker. Certainly the *name* Paul was associated with affection and excellence.

In his present life, a deep inner sadness had followed the death of his tiny baby girl in 1936—just three days of life. There had been something in him that had wanted to die, too. He had longed for that little one he'd never really known and had tried to quell this longing so that he could cope with the breakup of the first marriage.

In the midst of the melancholy memory, he could see the

pattern of unhappiness in the past. "James" had to leave his son Alan behind and had sobbed as he told the doctor, "I never saw him again." Later, as Jack Carstairs, he had two children, but had lost little baby Alice at birth. He must not have been ready yet. Had he done something, as Strages, that had brought no living children for hundreds of years? Was it because he had carelessly fathered several, as a soldier? Though Strages had the one he was proud of, Paul, he'd had several he never cared about. "What for?" he had asked. It made sense, from this pattern, that *all* children should have been prized.

At least now, inside, he knew that he loved and he was loved. And the love of the children that he had lost was not lost *forever.* He might well meet them again. Healing was coming, with the knowledge that he would live again—with opportunities to show how he had learned the values of love and family and courage.

In their little cottage, Al and Gladys often welcomed the children of the neighborhood who came by to talk with the man they knew was their friend.

RELIGION: "1. belief in a divine or superhuman power or powers to be obeyed and worshiped as the creator(s) and ruler(s) of the universe. 2. expression of this belief in conduct and ritual. 3 (a) any specific system of belief, worship, conduct, etc., often involving a code of ethics and a philosophy . . . (b) loosely, any system of beliefs, practices, ethical values, etc., resembling . . . such a system . . . "[3]

Religion or spirituality—this was the vital element, he knew now. He saw in those lives he'd gone from practically nothing to total immersion, from gazing at the stars to tightly structured ritual.

Religion for Solomon's manager of trade, Onon, was pragmatic, whatever was good for business; he laughed at any forecasts of an anointed Deliverer of the Jews.

Achmesh had met the man Jesus, but had not known He

was the Messiah, until he saw Him crucified. He had the average upbringing of a Jewish boy, but was upset by the merchandising going on in the temple. He had heard Jesus teach by the Sea of Galilee; had listened eagerly, could repeat much of what he heard, but admitted he didn't understand it all. Although declaring he was not a follower of Christ, the Hebrew was so taken over by His example and by the example of Stephen whom he called his friend that he went on to speak for Christ and to be crucified himself.

But the first one to call himself a Christian was the Roman soldier, Strages, who was "converted" by the Norse woman he married. He was ready to use his sword in a political/religious battle, to "Kill them all. Kill all the nonbelievers." When told by his interrogator that Christians should not approve of violence and bloodshed, he called the objections totally trivial. Asked about the resurrection, his response, "Resurrection of what?" showed he had no concept of it. Later, as Gregor, he recognized the need for suffering and, as Longo's friend, Wachwa, he knew the beauty and goodness of nature. Still, he had nothing but contempt for religious ritual.

Next he found himself completely involved in a ritualistic system, as the Dominican friar who in his old age joined the Jesuits. He could speak of hymns, recite prayers, but keep other parts of his order's works a secret. No involvement with other men and women was visible.

Ironic that his next experience was an offspring of the English king who was then the titular head of the Church of England, which had broken away under Henry VIII from the Catholic church. Not a legal son, either. His life style in no way reflected religious influence on character, but he did give some service to the Bible translators.

A true emotional experience came in the vision of Jesus for little Pierre.

A need to seek for union with God was first expressed in

his latest life as Jack Carstairs. Was this desire the fruit of those other experiences, to know more about God? Jack had enlisted "For God and Country" in the Union army. He had an emotional experience at his father's funeral in Richmond. He studied to be a minister at one point, but gave it up. Much later, he tried again; he spoke with the cardinal in Boston and was converted to Catholicism—with some reservations, however, after reading an extremely worldly book. Still, he knew he wanted this communion with God, wanted it more than anything. Was that why it happened, as he lay on his deathbed with his wife beside him, that he saw the angel on the ceiling—and just "walked off"?

Now it was making sense—healing sense!

He would trust in the universe, in the cosmos, in God. God was the Creator of everything. There was a kind of unspoken acceptance of the fact that Al was a traveler in a wilderness where directions were hard to find, that he was on a trail and parts of it would be rough and bumpy, would hurt and reopen old wounds. But it was understood: this trail that would lead through those wounds of earlier centuries and even past the scars in his present life, this trail would make him stronger for traveling it. Not physically, no doubt. But in the soul.

He found the page in Sugrue's *There Is a River* where he had underlined a passage in the chapter on philosophy:

> "Each soul enters the material plane not by chance, but through the grace, the mercy, of a loving Father; that the soul may, through its own choice, work out those faults, those fancies, which prevent its communion and at-onement with the Creative Forces . . .
>
> "As ye do unto the least of thy brethren, so ye do it unto thy Maker. These are laws . . . "[4]

But this was more than *laws*—this was his life!

14
Healing and Blessing

The sheer joy of being in Virginia Beach with the woman he loved was the crest-of-the-wave-of-healing feeling.

Al wrote to an artist friend the day after Christmas,[1] "'Tis good by oceanside here. Whistling winds around the house. No place on earth is more beautiful. Starting in January, something is in bloom always, 365 days a year, with cold weather sasanquas and daphnes out now—beautiful to paint."

Perhaps because of the Edenlike atmosphere, he found few customers for investments. He began studying for a real-estate license to add to other skills. As the grass and plants and trees began flourishing, he recalled the love of plants Jack Carstairs had. The hidden wish turned to action after Gladys said, "You have a way with flowers" and encouraged him to do something he really enjoyed.

Soon they had purchased a small greenhouse and set it up on the front lawn and stocked it with plants. He had an inspired name for the new business: "Glad Gardens." He sent out cheerful postcards, using the nickname friends and neighbors had for him: *"Smilin' Al* Offers: CARNATIONS, CANDYTUFT, GERANIUMS, PETUNIAS, COWSLIPS, SCARLET SAGE, ALYSSUM, PANSIES, AZALEAS," offering to plant them, "before the spring rush."

Al's personality began to bloom as well. Working with the flowers not only didn't tire him, it actually refreshed him. His smile became something of a trademark. With his broad grin, he'd offer his hand and a hearty "Happy Birthday!" The startled recipients would return a puzzled grin—and if it happened to be the actual birthday, they'd be even more puzzled. It raised a few eyebrows, but intrigued the growing circle of friends and customers.

"We're born again every day," Al happily explained to everyone who asked him about it, "and we have a new opportunity every day, so why not say 'Happy Birthday'?" They'd shake their heads, smiling and agreeing in spite of themselves.

He didn't explain to everyone that Gladys and his friends knew, as he knew, that he had already been born several times and expected to go right on being born anew, life after life, until he reached the Goal.

Al's cheerfulness was reaching an ever-growing circle. Star of the Sea Catholic Church was across the street from Glad Niche, and a home for the nuns was almost adjacent to the vines and fig trees Al had cultivated. He loved the feeling of living those happy words from Micah 4:4: "But they shall sit every man under his vine and under his fig tree; and none shall make them afraid . . . " As the nuns passed back and forth along the path near his vines and fig trees, Al with a mischievous twinkle in his eye would blithely greet each one, "Happy Birthday, Sister!" At first they were flustered and did not know what to make of it, but eventually they began to smile and return the greeting.

Even the priest of Star of the Sea, Father Habets, regularly exchanged greetings with Al and Gladys. Al's greetings and cards were sometimes more humorous than one might consider proper, but the prelate wrote his thanks " . . . for the funniest birthday card ever seen. Not that I mind my age—seventy-one—I'm rather proud of it—but you are so loyal not to give away a secret. I have enjoyed twelve happy years with you as neighbors. God bless you!"

One of Al's great delights was talking with the young children in the neighborhood, as well as Gladys's little nephew Michael. The tots swarmed around Glad Niche as bees around the gardenias.

When a child spied Al by his greenhouse, the cry would go up, "Mr. Flower Man! Mr. Flower Man!" Al would respond with a quick smile. He found a natural love for children, one he had never been able to express before. For the first time—in any of his lives—he had many happy children around. Gladys described how he was with them: "He taught them about nature, to understand it and respect it. He had been saddened when some children tore the leaves off our mimosa tree and it died. Instead of yelling and scolding, Al explained to the children about how plants grow, how to take care of them so they bear fruit. From time to time he would give them some, such as the figs or grapes. They really learned from him—and never harmed the plants again."

One child in particular, little Walter, would toddle over from his home along the side of the lake to see "Mr. Flower Man" and just talk about anything and everything. At first his mother wondered where he was and would come out and call him—but soon she, too, stopped for a visit with "Mr. Flower Man." Al felt unusually drawn to little Walter. His alert, affectionate ways and the look in his eyes were both warm and familiar. Was it possible Al had known him before? Testing a theory, Al used "Paul" in his conversation a few times. Each time, Walter responded as if that were his name. Al confided only to Gladys that it was a beautiful feeling that his brother Paul might have come back to share affection.

Another change which set him off as an oddball among those who knew him only casually was his outward increase in humility, "trying to lose the ego," going so far as to stop using the capital "I" for himself when writing letters; he substituted the small, lower case "i."

But the greatest change was the genuine happiness that became as much a part of him as his skin. The heavier worries, the economic struggle, the physical problems, no longer bothered him. They existed, yes. In 1958, he had a fifth heart attack and a mild stroke. But these problems were no longer the heavy actors on his daily stage, as they had been; instead they were bit players, trivial matters he would handle. One way or another, he did. Not just his own problems, either. If someone he knew had a difficulty where he could help—whether an A.R.E. friend, a fellow worker at the Norfolk Post Office, an inmate in a prison, a nephew in personal crisis, a waitress serving their table—Al would do it. With a smile.

He added a couple of beehives to the gardens. One acquaintance asked what a man of his obvious scholarly background was doing tending flowers and raising bees. With a warm smile, Al answered, "It's one of the easiest ways to spread beauty and love!" But the words and their implications set him to musing while he worked. When he went back in the house, he sat down at his typewriter and tapped out:

> "So long as the bee is outside the petals of the flower, it buzzes and emits sounds. But when it is inside the

flower, the sweetness thereof has silenced and overpowered the bee. Forgetful of sounds and itself, it drinks the nectar in quiet.

"Men of learning, you, too, are making a noise in the world. But know, the moment you get the slightest enjoyment of the sweetness . . . you will be like the bee in the flower, inebriated with the nectar of divine love.

"Are too many people in the world making noises when flowers of silence are countless blessings around us?"

God had helped him find the right place, at the right time: this wonderful, spiritual, loving wife; their home with its atmosphere of blessing; the Association for Research and Enlightenment, where he later was able to lead groups in classes of shared spiritual study; a job at the Norfolk Post Office, somewhat steadier than real estate had been; and the Virginia Beach Friends Meeting, where love and worship were shared with friends.

The progress of the healing seemed to be happily set. Al used many daily meditations, a favorite of which he typed up, set on the wall by his bed, and re-read each morning:

"THIS IS THE DAY WHICH THE LORD HATH MADE;

"LET US BE GLAD AND REJOICE IN IT."—Psalm 118:24

"May this day be bright and beautiful in every way for me. May every hour hold happiness; may every experience of this day be enriching and rewarding. May every person I meet this day receive a blessing from me and leave a blessing with me.

"May this day hold for me healing. May I know and feel the wonderful healing power of God, mighty and strong within me. May this day I feel filled with life and health and strength. May I radiate a blessing of health and healing to others this day; may all those persons around me be helped and healed through my healing faith.

"May this day be a growth for me, a day in which I see myself as a child of God learning and progressing and growing on the path of life. May this day be a day of appreciation by me of all that has gone before, of all the ways in which I have learned to grow; a day of appreciation by me of all the blessings that are right at hand, the good that surrounds me constantly, *always*. Bless me this day, to THY service, in making others happy."

Pushing himself toward further spiritual disciplines, in the beginning of 1961 he decided to try "living" the Sermon on the Mount, taking one thought to focus on, a day at a time, and to keep a journal of the results.

Among the daily notes, January 12, Matthew 5:5, "Blessed are the meek: for they shall inherit the earth," he wrote, "Everything 'right' happened for and to me today. Found that this verse was marvelous in supplanting negative thoughts."

For February 13, he had chosen Matthew 6:19, "Lay not up for yourselves treasures upon earth, where moth and rust doth corrupt, and where thieves break through and steal . . . " But he never got to apply that verse.

Instead, a total collapse. He was rushed to the hospital, victim of a severe stroke, unable to speak, unable to even move. He could hear; he could move his eyes.

Could he have heard an echo of the master's voice when he was in trance?

"The experiences given were to teach the soul to rely not on the house of the body but completely to rely on the universal . . . that the soul is making its way back and that the body should help—and not dictate."

It was, he felt, as if the universal, as if God, had said to him, "You think you have made a lot of progress. Well, you've had a long way to go. Let's give you a *real* test."

There was no way now that the body could dictate.

But depression did not take over. Within him were those vivid memories, the knowledge and experience of feeling all those different personalities. He knew the Spirit was working within him. If he got better, fine. If not, there would probably be a decent physical existence next time, perhaps like the one he had after the icy life as Gregor. But he wanted to stay *here*, now, with Gladys. Slowly, one muscle at a time, one joint at a time, he began regaining the ability to move. Gladys's daily visits inspired him. His speech began returning. Even the doctor was ready to reverse his original prediction and admit that Al might not be permanently wheelchair-bound.

A bit over two months later, toward the end of April, he was able to return home. Unlike earlier illnesses, this time a torrent of cards and warm wishes flowed in, bringing added strength with each one.

Previously he had felt reluctant to accept gifts and kindnesses; now he realized that though he was trying to be humble, he was denying the giver pleasure. It had been a mistake. As he explained to his niece, "Since it is more blessed to give than to receive, the person who receives is actually *helping the giver* to be more blessed!"

To Gladys, he mentioned wryly that he had found "one good thing this stroke has done: now I really have to depend on the spirit and not the body."

Something—was it the spirit?—got the body to respond. He began a shuffling recovery, then came the day he could lift himself from the recliner chair, then use a cane to go to the next room by himself.

Now Gladys encouraged him to come to work with her each morning when she drove to A.R.E. headquarters. Al had a small desk in a partially open wire enclosure amusingly called "the chicken coop," where he could write and research, culling quotations from and about the Bible and other subjects. Because it was partially open to the corridor, people passing to other basement offices could see him and many would stop for a brief moment of peaceful conversation. (So he wouldn't get too tired, they arranged for a canvas cot to be set up beside the desk in the corner.)

His body might be slow, but his happy disposition wasn't. Seeing the librarian, Charlotte, passing by, he invited her to pause for a moment, not knowing how she needed some understanding at that moment. Her husband of thirty-seven years had just broken the news that he was leaving her. She said she was returning to Philadelphia. Al wrote to his Philadelphia friend, Wilmer Alice Adams, who shortly after telephoned Charlotte and invited her to dinner. In a few days, she introduced Charlotte to a friend, Birley Schoen, who emphasized that he was a confirmed bachelor. That was fine, Charlotte said, because she herself was just learning how good it felt to be independent. Two years later they were married.

Gladys reminded Al that he had written an article for the A.R.E. *Searchlight* on the topic, "Is Reincarnation in the Bible?" after his earlier (1958) hospitalization, and he could do some more research on that and on other favorite topics such as The Revelation.

It wasn't hard for Al to get fired up. He heard an acquaintance saying that belief alone was enough to get one into heaven and that reincarnation was some kind of fictional myth. Others thought the same thing. He got out the little typewriter to put his own feelings on paper. He had been struggling with more determination than he had ever known he possessed, because he knew now that it was worth every ounce of effort.

He wrote a passionate denial that all the virtues were

summarized in one word, *belief.* "If that be true," he wrote, "there would be no reason for His coming . . . is it sensible to believe that Jesus contradicted all His pronouncements on the values of piety and moral life . . . by stating . . . it was all right to believe and then sin all you want? Yet this is actually what many people think! . . .

"Some people think that saying a word, just a tiny word like 'believe' or 'abracadabra' will open the gates of heaven and make physical death the doorway to eternal life without ever having to abide by the biblical truths! These people should be asked to prove that reincarnation is *not.* All who tap their own individual sources of eternal truths know and do not have to prove to themselves what a truth is. The very fact that a person challenges reincarnation in the Bible indicates that person's desire for an easier way. For reincarnation is *not* an easy way."

He knew.

Before his trip into past lives, Al's days had been often tiring concerns, energy enough to get done what had to be done—then try to recuperate.

But after the studies and the healing experience, in spite of the heart attack in 1958 (his fifth) and the severe stroke three years later, he was not only writing, researching, but actively working with people as well. (He was better off than Jack Carstairs, who had lost his right arm in a mill accident and stayed home, depressed, afterward.) But whether it was the glad atmosphere in the home or the meditations or the experiences as he often led the noon meditations at the A.R.E. headquarters or all of these—he became aware of a spiritual vigor which seemed somehow to grow as it was used. Even in the mid-sixties he would take part in the Search for God programs and lead discussion groups on the Bible and the readings.

He was adding new skills to the ones already shown in the stained glass of the past; none of them, as far as Al could recall, had demonstrated much writing ability. Or even writing effort. Working as a leader with groups seemed to be new, also. He had been just a participant, as the black singer; just a member of the tribe, as Gregor. It gave him a start to wonder if this ability to lead could possibly have come from Captain Strages of the Roman army? Something *good* from that arrogant man?

There was another element in conflict in the past: fighting versus peace. Al had joined that peace-working group, the Society of Friends. He had the time now for research. By midsummer he had completed an eight-page article, "Cry Not, 'Peace, Peace,' " which became the feature of the September 1962 *Searchlight.* Based on the Cayce readings for the achievement of a new order of peace in the world, it took its title from reading 694-2, "Cry not 'Peace, Peace' when thou, thyself, hast not *shown* peace to thy brethren!" (In Jeremiah 6:14 and 8:11, "They have healed also the hurt of the daughter of my people slightly, saying Peace, peace; when there is no peace.") In the article Al emphasized his belief that "the *living* of Christ's teachings would save the world, rather than attacking in any way, because the cause of war is fear and hatred within the human heart."

Of course, this took effort, tremendous effort. He did have new energy but it was not inexhaustible.

But when there was a task which needed a concentration of energy, he would somehow find the strength sufficient for the task. Whenever he felt he could help a friend, he would dredge up the means from somewhere.

One dark summer night, well after midnight, there was a knock at the side door of the cottage. His niece, who had been visiting, was sleeping in the guest room at Glad Niche; she heard the knock, threw on a robe, and opened the door. There were three young people in their teens—one a friend's daughter—who explained that they had been so wrapped up in talking and singing folk songs down town that they had forgotten the time. Now all the buses to the distant area where they were staying had stopped running. Would she mind? The niece offered to drive them *if* she could find the way.

In moments, the sound of shuffling and the tap of a cane and Al's sleepy voice: "What is the problem?" After some discussion, it turned out that Al was the only one really familiar with the area where they needed to go; rather than give directions, he insisted on going with them to be sure they reached their house safely. Not a word of reprimand or protest, but a matter-of-fact statement that he could help and he would.

Unable to do much physically besides getting from one room to another with his cane, Al nevertheless did a tremendous variety of writing and correspondence. He would nominate people he admired for awards and recognition. One such person was Hugh Lynn Cayce, whom Al nominated for First Citizen of Virginia Beach in January of 1964. He wrote a letter, citing many reasons, to the First Citizen Committee, closing with what he thought was the most powerful reason: "He truly lives the Sermon on the Mount, in the Bible, given us by Jesus. There is hardly a person in Virginia Beach, either from youth or from church work or from many other ways, who has not been affected for good, directly or indirectly, by Hugh Lynn Cayce."

Al was delighted to hear that Hugh Lynn would indeed receive the honor. Ironically, on the night of its presentation, Gladys and Al could not attend the dinner because Gladys was ill.

He wrote about Gladys for the *Reader's Digest*'s "Most Unforgettable Character" essay and was sad that it was never printed.

He wrote to and for the Quaker group working against capital punishment. Al believed life was a precious gift—and as long as one has it, one can grow spiritually even if the body is in a prison. After all, he had experienced how a person could do many things by mistake, could even kill just because he or she was told to, and he also knew that prayers could work.

But, as he said to one young man in prison, "Prayers are always answered but they may be delayed. Prayers are always a two-way street, fifty percent depends upon the prayee, the one prayed for, the receiver, who can delay by not receiving. You have been in my prayers, so receive, because love is being sent you constantly." He reminded the youth, "After all, the foundation of the Christian church was startled when St. Paul was in jail more than once."

He explained "our only purpose in living, in coming into this incarnation, is to help others. We may go here and there to find people to help. But in jail one doesn't have to go anywhere. They are all there, as many as one wants to help, they are there, waiting to be helped, crying to be helped, and you are there!"

From his own life he could add, "After all, the body is a prison, everything is a prison *if* one considers it such. But wherever you are, or anyone is, is an opportunity, and when one can turn stumbling blocks into stepping-stones, one can turn so-called misfortunes into opportunities . . . Please help those over there who need you; you know so much more than they do. We have to take advantage of *all* opportunities, or else we have to come back life after life, and meet the same opportunities again . . . "

He followed his own advice, taking every opportunity to help. He had been out of touch with his sister, Ruth, for many years since she had a divorce and a nervous breakdown. When he found out she was in St. Elizabeth's Hospital in Washington, he spoke with Gladys and they arranged to bring Ruth to visit at the little cottage for two weeks each summer. Ruth, who had felt anonymous in the institution and long since given up her art, when she was surrounded by gentleness and love, began to paint again. She worked toward recalling the skills she had developed when studying art in Paris. She left a fresh painting with Al and Gladys after each visit. One was a shimmering impression of Al among the flowers in the greenhouse.

At this point he found a special pleasure in getting in touch and keeping in touch with old and new friends. One friend said of him, "Al's circle of friends and acquaintances is so wide, and his familiarity with each one's needs and abilities so accurate, that it's a hobby for him to help them fill each other's needs!"

One evening when he was out to dinner with Gladys at their favorite restaurant, he asked their waitress why she seemed a bit sad. She confided that her boyfriend had lost his job. Two weeks later, Gladys reported that the waitress spotted them and hurried over. "Thank you for talking to that man, Mr. Turner! Joe went to see him like you suggested and now he has a better job than the old one. You are a saint!"

Al shook his head. "Far from it! But I'm so glad that it worked out." As she left, he confided to Gladys, "It is such a pleasure to be able to do that."

Gladys understood. Al thrived on helping people. But as he continued his activities, she worried that he might go too far. "You know you're not supposed to overdo."

"I'm afraid I'll underdo," he said with a grin. If he had an opportunity and the strength to fill it, he would. He enjoyed leading discussion groups and was glad to be asked to lead the noontime meditation periodically.

Physically he was never entirely out of the woods, but his personality seemed to stay in the sun. Albert Turner's trip into past lives had resulted in more than a healing experience for his personality, his character, we could even say his higher self; there was the companion experience of bringing the skills of other selves to the foreground and developing new ones. The soul that the Master said was finding its way back would not have so far to go.

Sixteen years after his past-life discoveries, after years of work and study and happiness, Al was hospitalized and, following a brain hemorrhage, passed through "God's other door," in Edgar Cayce's words, on June 27, 1968.

When the memorial service was held, the many friends coming past the tall pines to the entrance of the Virginia Beach Friends Meeting marveled at the full blooms on the gardenia bushes, spreading their brilliant sweetness into the fragrant air. Those bushes, which Al had planted out of love, had never bloomed so early before. Warm and happy tributes were spoken, tributes that would hardly have fit the tense and worried man who had first come to Virginia Beach, the man who had asked Dr. George if he could help him learn from his past lives.

The memorial booklet closed with a poem by Albert's friend and A.R.E. member Juliet Brooke Ballard, reprinted from *The A.R.E. Journal*, Summer, 1968. The last verse summed it up:

> Your way lies open to the stars;
> And now we speed you on your way.
> Waiting the time you will return
> To guide us on a brighter day.[2]

15
Exploring Karmic Possibilities

Instead of treating karma like the weather—lots of people talking about it, but few doing anything about it—let us examine what we can see of it and find out what there is to learn from it—karma in Al's life and in our own lives.

Karma has been explained in many ways, commonly as a "tit for tat" by fate. Its original meaning is summed up in *The Oxford English Dictionary* (Oxford and New York, 1989):

"*Karma.* Also *karman* [Sanskrit, *karma, karman,* action, fate]. In Buddhism, the sum of a person's actions in one of his successive states of existence, regarded as determining his fate in the next; hence, necessary fate or destiny, following as effect from cause. Also in Hinduism."

Some people say that it is like that law of physics: "For every action there is an equal and opposite reaction." Hard and fast, as arid and sere as statistics. "An eye for an eye and a tooth for a tooth"[1] is the elementary example of karmic judgment in the Bible.

In Al's life, karma was not glimpsed in its living color until after he studied everything he could recall from the nine lifetimes and carefully searched for links that might be cause and effect.

But we did not see the "eye for an eye" take place, in part because none of his deeds were visibly outrageous—at least none of the ones he described to Dr. Henry George. Unlike horrible crimes recently in the newspapers, he did not talk of torturing anyone or cutting out someone's heart.

There may have been far more contained in Al's lives than the doctor's questions brought out. Allowing for that possibility, we will consider the main actions that seemed to bring karmic effects in later lives:

- From the short flashback of Onon's life, the karmic provocation seems to be his ignoring the possibility of a miracle, of a promised Deliverer; laughing at a sacred promise. *Karmic result: he met and died for the Deliverer.*
- The Jew seemed to have few faults; it appeared reasonable for him to call Pilate "that monkey the emperor sent down" and to hate the Romans with vehemence. *He became what he hated.*
- The Roman captain was the kind of soldier who always did what he was told and accepted corruption as part of army life. He didn't even seem to hate his enemies, just killed them. He slept with several women before he married one and had a child he was proud of. *He was to get lost from his tribe/family and die. No children.*
- Gregor, the Siberian, didn't realize he needed to stay with his tribe; he heard a master's advice, tried to understand, got lost, and froze to death. *His next life held warmth and ease and friends.*
- Wachwa, after childhood as a slave, lived with Longo and friends, wanting no women, no ritual, until killed by a

shark. *He was to live celibate, with ritual.*

• The friar followed his order, prayed and worked, properly righteous. *He was to be a king's son, lose a lover and son, help with scriptures.*

• James ran from home, didn't have the guts to escape his father's men, so abandoned his sweetheart and child, but worked on the Bible later. *He was to be a drowning child, but see Jesus.*

• Pierre lived briefly and died. *He was to live a full life with a family.*

• Jack had a good childhood, a youth as a soldier, married, worked, wanted to study spiritually, had one living child, died, saw an angel. *And returned as Al with a need to make spiritual sense of life.*

Nothing horrifying. Nothing glorious. Nothing sickening or vicious. Not, at least, in what he told. He saw the bloody mess that was Stephen, but never went into detail about what was done to him when he, himself, was crucified. As Captain Slaughter, he seemed uninterested in descriptions; killing was just killing. There was barely a mention of the shark biting off the leg in the Mediterranean. Still, there could be pain without violence. No violence was mentioned when young James was taken away by his father's men and forced to leave his sweetheart and his son, but the sobs in the recorded voice were real. No remarkable horror stories—but plenty to learn.

These seem to sum up his lessons:

1. Don't laugh at the concept of a miracle.
2. Make choices based on love. Waste no energy on hate.
3. Value women and children. Force often fails.
4. Stay connected with the clan. Hear the inner voice.
5. Value women. Don't despise worship ritual.
6. Ritual can help, but not fulfill.
7. Value women. Love without responsibility makes victims.

8. Even a victim can see Christ.
9. God is there and aware. Search inside.

By the end of the tenth life, Al showed he had learned to honor women; Gladys, he said, was the most spiritual being. His five heart attacks and two strokes forced him to see that the body could help and not dictate. For him, the karmic factors— mild as they were compared to others— were the steps of the ladder, and he could feel the happiness as he climbed.

Clients seeking help from professionals today often are looking for relief from a symptom or condition, not for an understanding of karmic relationships. When the problem is not relieved by working within the present life, however, the healer has to search further. Then we may expect evidence of karma to appear. Thousands of recorded successes[2] indicate that healing comes on release of the causing event or events, along with reconciliation, forgiveness of others and the self. The word "karma" doesn't even have to be spoken for the law to work.

Some psychologists' casebooks have far more gruesome recollections than Al's; they illustrate all types of sexual abuse, physical and mental violence, mutilation, and torture. Of course, there are beautiful experiences, too, but the ones causing the trouble are not the happy memories. These old experiences remain alive in the unconscious or subconscious—to use a fairy-tale simile—like some elf that lives in its host-castle, crouching there as an unseen part of the castle family, but still capable of producing fear or mischief, disability or conflicting urges in the personality, until it can be found and released.

On the need for working it out, Dr. Judith Miller, transpersonal psychologist, says that in her experience with clients, when knowledge of happenings in past lives comes up, sometimes it is pleasant, but other times it includes tragic or terrible echoes of a past event, echoes which affect the present. This knowledge has been hidden within the body, in the deep part of the being.

Dr. Miller believes it is important to act on these uncovered findings, to work them out; they are part of the life story, and if they are not worked out, they will keep on contributing tension and repeating their part in the play.

Because the body and the mind/spirit are so intimately connected, she adds, when this knowledge comes to light, there is often an emotional, spiritual, and *physical* releasing of those hidden memories.

After one client's deep release, the young woman felt many symptoms, as the body itself went through the elimination of the traumatic memories—as if they were bodily waste. There were other physical symptoms of the catharsis, and muscle reactions as well. The client was truly "purged." And felt cleansed of the past.

"Working it out" does not mean making the memory totally vanish, of course, because all we have lived and felt is a part of us. It does mean defusing it, letting off its steam, removing its power to hurt because we know it's out, it is not an active part of us any more, it is over and done with.

Psychiatrist Denys Kelsey, whose wife, Joan Grant, author of *Far Memory*, often worked with him in searching clients' past lives, related one case of an Englishman who had a horror of feathers, could not use or even touch a feather pillow, for example. When he was regressed, he found himself in the Foreign Legion, in a desert battle. When they had to retreat, orders were not to leave any wounded alive for fear they might be tormented or mangled by desert beasts. He was wounded and helpless; they thought he was dead and just left him. Vultures dropped from the sky onto his face, his neck, any exposed part. No wonder he had a horror of feathers! Brought back to the present, he found tremendous relief now that the cause was known to be in the past. He even purchased an unplucked chicken at a market and carried it happily home for dinner. He was free at last.

Dr. Gina Cerminara, who wrote *Many Mansions* and *The World Within*, the ground-breaking books on psychically discovered past lives from the Edgar Cayce readings, speaks of several types of karma, such as "mockery karma," "boomerang karma," "symbolic karma," and "organismic karma," as kinds of physical reactions to past misdeeds. For an example of mockery karma, a man who had made fun of a cripple in a past life was crippled by polio; an example of symbolic karma was one who had brought about a bloody revolution in a past experience had become severely anemic in the present. A malfunction of an organ of the body, with some link to former deeds or cruelty, she called "organismic." For instance, a child who had seemingly incurable incontinence, unresponsive to many physicians for years, was found by the readings to have been a man whose task had been to repeatedly duck the victim of witchcraft trials in water, usually until drowning followed. The advice was to suggest to the youth as he was falling asleep that he was good and kind, that he would help other people. The next day was the first time in nine years he had not wet the bed. The mother continued the suggestions for several months; the problem never returned.

Whether or not a physical problem today is a result of karma cannot be answered without a knowledge of one's past lives. Sometimes, there may be an entirely different reason for the problem. Dr. Cerminara reports that some past-life readings said that the misfortune was purely accidental.

Of course, we recall, when his disciples (who apparently were aware of past-life karmic effects) asked Jesus, "Master, who did sin, this man, or his parents, that he was born blind?" Jesus told them, "Neither hath this man sinned, nor his parents: but that the works of God should be made manifest in him."[3]

Some physical problems can be induced by our own attitudes and in that sense might be considered karmic, although not from the past lives but from the present.

Indications of repressed feelings, for example, often show in the body-mind connection. Dr. C. Norman Shealy, when speaking at an A.R.E. symposium, gave a number of examples of these in present lives, such as clients who developed a backache when they repressed an urge to tell someone else, "Get off my back," or developed an ulcer when they said of someone, "He makes me sick." Such results are more than just symbolic.

To those who lack confidence in information acquired psychically (by the Edgar Cayce readings, for example), it might be informative to know that over 14,000 records at the A.R.E. attest to the high percentage of accuracy and help they gave. Psychologists and psychiatrists working with past-life information acquired directly from an individual by hypnosis find many cases similar to those of Dr. Cerminara. Their casebooks indicate excellent records of cures, once the causes are revealed.

The label of "mockery karma" could readily apply to two of Al's sequence: Onon mocking Solomon's suggestion of a Deliverer and Achmesh mocking Pontius Pilate and hating the Roman military. When Onon became Achmesh, he personally met and died on behalf of the Deliverer, and when he became Strages, he lived as a bastard Roman soldier.

There was nothing among his cases as simple as Dr. Cerminara's "boomerang" karma, next-life retribution in kind, but we do see possible delayed retribution for his taking women when a Roman soldier: in the Tripolitan life with no women, and the friar's celibate existence as well.

We do need to note that, although most of the events we tend to associate with karma are unpleasant, it is not only not all bad, but can be mentally and physically rewarding. In fact, Al had some delightful experiences one could call karmic. The life by the Mediterranean Sea was pleasant in every way—except for the tragic childhood, with affectionate friends and appreciation of nature, the sun and moon and stars given to them by the Maker. And his life as Jack had pleasures, especially in childhood—memories of spring strawberries, his favorite horse—and even some pleasures as an adult—with a pretty and loving wife, and Chopin's music. He did lose an arm in the mill, at the end, but there doesn't seem enough evidence to say it was karmic. It could have been just an accident—but handling it without bitterness would strengthen his character.

Dr. Roger Woolger, Jungian psychotherapist, in *Other Lives, Other Selves,* discusses karma in some depth. He notes that both men and women clients often find they have experienced lives as the opposite sex. Because Al never listed a feminine side—although he said in trance that he might have had one but did not remember it—it is helpful to know that having qualities of both genders adds dimensions to personality. We may indeed have both a man and a woman in our multidimensional psyche, with the stronger figure making decisions. Dr. Woolger noted there are often reversals, so a male part of the personality can experience what the female feels. It is sometimes a painful teaching experience. One case was a woman, fearful of sex, who recalled a past life as a woman raped and mutilated by soldiers. This explained her fear. But even further back, she recalled other lives as a cruel soldier who inflicted just such pain on his women victims!

While assisting clients, who may be both victims and aggressors in the past, to uncover the buried rage, Dr. Woolger points out, "Not just the victim, but the bully and the rapist in all of us also are in need of healing and forgiveness."[4] Self-forgiveness is vital in healing.

Whether or not we react in this life to the same individuals we have harmed or helped in the past—a question not easily settled unless the other party is willing to be regressed and identified—what really matters is our ability to understand what we did and what was done to us and to forgive. In fact it seems, from countless cases, that those phrases from the Lord's Prayer freely rendered as "Forgive us our sins as we forgive those who have sinned against us" can have a powerful effect on future lives.

The emotions felt in the regressions, the guilt and rage and grief that surface in the experiencing, are the same as if the other party were there and it was happening again. They are *real.* The release and healing, then, are also real.

It seems crystal clear that we will have to work out the karmic relationships with those individuals sooner or later.

This karmic principle is behind the vital but not yet well-known work with the growing Victim-Offender Reconciliation Program, known acronymically as VORP,[5] which began in Canada in 1974, inspired by Mennonite probation officers. It was begun in the U.S. in Illinois three years later. Victims and offenders meet face to face, each learning about the other, working out restitution. At first working only with minor cases, it now has some groups quietly working with violent cases such as homicide. But with murder cases, the victim's family member does not meet the actual offender in *their* case, but an offender who committed the same crime against a different person. Still, the emotions felt are real and the release has been a true catharsis.

I met one of the offenders, who is serving a life sentence in Graterford Prison where I am a volunteer tutor. He spoke quietly but with strong emotion about how he now has a far different realization of what he did. Criminologist Julia Hall, Ph.D., says she has seen awakening understanding and often relief for the victims, who had sometimes not realized crimes are often results of panic or accident. And she has seen a whole-hearted change in attitude on the part of offenders. Though they may never return to the "outside," their lives and thinking have been changed.

Knowing, feeling, and understanding what happened in past lives is part of a similar process, with the goal of learning the basic shortcomings and working to remedy them. Forgiving and being forgiven. It seems to bring benefits even when the people we meet today are not the same ones we injured—or who injured us.

But sometimes they may be.

Though it seems a small part of the past, I clearly remember the incident I relived as a medieval printer and the stabbing ordered by the politician I had criticized. A dozen years ago I believe I found out who he was. I had written a stinging criticism of this man, prominent in circles opposing recognition of psychic phenomena; it was printed in an intellectual magazine. He read it, phoned, and berated me as ignorant, uneducated, and much more. Recalling the stabbing of the past, instead of firing back anything similar, I examined one of his books on the subject, found and noted forty errors in one chapter, and enclosed the list with a mild letter suggesting he had probably drawn his conclusions from some harm done by a pseudo-psychic. Only silence followed.

In Al's past relationships, he did not show that any of the people he had harmed—he must have killed many as a soldier—had turned up in a later life to exact retribution. But the interrogator did not ask him that question. Perhaps, in a karmic view of killing, the Jews who he said crucified him as Achmesh were involved in the other side of the battles he fought as a Roman soldier, but this is only supposition.

It is reasonable to think that individuals who might have injured us in a past life would show up as those we would be able to mistreat or injure in this one, and the reverse—that those we had harmed might be in a position to cause us harm today. But it is rare to hear about. More often, we hear of cases where neighbors or family members or even communities with relationships return during the same period. A fascinating and most extraordinary example is that of a group of Californians who, separately, under hypnosis, recalled living in a village in Civil War Virginia with their past-life names and homes—much of which has been checked and found accurate. The story is featured in *Venture Inward* (September/October 1993).[6]

There well may be evidence for group karma, but without far wider research we can only speculate from what we have learned. That may be behind the historical swings from one form of tyranny to another, from some example of political mayhem to a nationwide plague. One wonders why there were so many babies deformed by the popular use of the drug Thalidomide by pregnant women shortly after World War II.

Two major ways in which past lives seem to be influencing current behavior include, according to Dr. Woolger, (1) "realizing these characters from the past are recognizable as other 'selves' that have always been deep in the background of our consciousness, and (2) that this character's past-life story is somehow being reenacted in this life and remains unfinished."[7]

Each life in the series is part of another self. With help, we can see many selves, all nesting within us, often deep inside. It is a challenge to find and identify the "unfinished business" but well worth the effort, for if that is the basis of the recurring problem, we can get the actors to conclude that scene and move off stage so the rest of the drama may continue.

Discovering "unfinished business" for ourselves is discussed in the appendix. It is worthwhile mentioning it here, however, because it is usually not a quick process, although some of the examples given may make it seem so. What is important is the learning and then "working it out," which can be tried on our own or with a professional. Successful work with professionals—physicians, psychologists, psychiatrists licensed by an accrediting agency—has been reported in many thousands of cases.

Clients have found, after a series of lives was identified, that blocks were removed, phobias vanished, nightmares left, once they identify and release the traumatic happenings that were hidden in their past. Those working on their own may also succeed, with luck, in identifying past-life problems and working them out, but if any deep emotions are aroused, reexperiencing them may be frightening. Usually the individual's other self will be alert enough to halt the process if it is beginning to hurt. A therapist not well trained might let the experience continue before the client was ready for it.

We are dealing, of course, with human beings in developing stages, human beings who are thought to have minds and destinies of their own. Children learn from what happens to them what they can expect next time in the same situation, if their parents are consistent. If adults are going to learn from what happens to them, most cannot look to a parent for training as they might have done when children.

We are also too literal minded, too filled with complexes, inner drives, and uncertainties, to wrap our guidelines all in "Love thy neighbor as thyself." The concept of karma can bring relief with its promise of balance—if not in the present life, certainly in the series of lives—especially since we may have several selves within us with differing goals, as Dr. James Fadiman explained with personal multiplicities.

Studies such as those by Dr. William Tiller add pieces to the puzzle of who and where we are and where we are going. He has evidence of consciousness (less intellectual might call it "spirit") in all of matter, very much as did the ancient Greeks.[8] This fits well with the puzzle pieces Dr. Fadiman contributes when he speaks of individuals claiming they are receiving messages from objects—perhaps a neon sign or an aquarium would give this client of his a message. His criterion for considering the message was not "Who sent it, where did it come from?" but "Is it helpful?" Remembering that psychics may often pick up information from sources that are not apparent to the rest of us, it might be wiser to study the "self" that is picking up the information rather than dismiss it out of hand. Surely karma works with psychics as much as with the average person.

The more we see of the workings of karmic law and the results over time, the more hope there is that by exploring the troubled selves and the happy selves, we will gain the knowledge to "work it out" on our own stage, one of our "actors" at a time.

The karmic swings, the changes up and down in circumstances and relationships, appear to be a universal law which seems to fit right in with "the law and the prophets."

Dr. Gina Cerminara gave an excellent overview of karma in *Many Mansions* and explained that deep-lying and sometimes contradictory urges in the unconscious, which we must learn to redeem, is a concept of cardinal importance in reincarnationist psychology and may shed light on several areas. Foreshadowing the conclusions of many today, she suggested that contradictory urges might suggest a possible solution to the problems of multiple personality.

The contrast between looking at one's self and looking at a series of lives is that with the latter we can see how the actions of a person's mind and spirit in the past can create an effect which carries forward to our present and future. We can see the many selves nesting deep within us—each with a different personality component, yet all in some way connected. We are happiest when these selves do not contend with each other but work in harmony.

Recognizing and learning from the connections and their results is the way to work with the karma, which in turn appears to set off other signals around us, showing that we are in a far wider world than we originally imagined.

We may find meaning in apparently unrelated happenings occurring close together, indicating that there is *something* bringing that connection to our attention. "Synchronicity" is the term given to a set of events happening together which are not related as cause and effect. Alan Vaughn described, as an example, watching the bow of a canoe through some bushes as it passes on a lake, then seeing the stern follow. The bow does not *cause* the stern, but something is *connecting* them.

What do karma and synchronicity have to do with each other? Karma comes from the Buddhist and Hindu concepts: action by a force called Fate, balancing elements of our successive existences. "Synchronicity" comes from the Greek and is loosely defined as a "meaningful coincidence."

As we struggle to find where we are with our karma, it is often helpful to keep our eyes open for happenings that are synchronistic. Apparently guided by a force that knows what we are doing and how we feel, these happenings can manifest as playful or even lifesaving. According to psychologist Dr. Judith Miller, such occurrences are a part of the process. Often the events are solid, visible, with a physical connection.

One example: Ann had a friend who had gone to Paris. One day she saw a model of the Eiffel Tower in a store window; next, a billboard advertising a French film; in the restaurant where she ate lunch the music included "April in Paris." Her friend, whom she hadn't seen for a month, almost literally bumped into her as she came out of the restaurant.

Another example: Janice was driving to meet her friend, Lew, in a restaurant. Lew had earlier suggested that some of her plans were too far out, that she was like a balloon and needed someone to hold the string to keep her down to earth. On her way, she saw a pink balloon by the side of the road, probably let go by some disappointed child in a passing car. For the humor of it, she stopped the car, took in the balloon, and proceeded to the restaurant. In there she found Lew with a blue helium balloon—which he had found with its string tangled in a bush as he had walked to the cafe.

Another "coincidence" —this one could have ended in death, but didn't—happened to me on a rainy Sunday night as I was driving home from central Philadelphia. About to enter the Schuylkill Expressway, I saw the car ahead of me slow down a couple of times, then pick up speed as it swung onto the right lane of traffic near the 30th Street Station, actually a junction of lanes. Sure that now it would come up to speed, I swung in behind it, but it stopped short—and in the rain, though I braked, I could not stop before I bumped it. Meanwhile, a horde of cars was passing us. That car, with two women in it, pulled over onto a narrow island separating the main road from the other part of the junction. I followed, stopped, put my car in park, got out, and walked up to their car. The two women got out, examined the back of their car, and agreed there was no real damage, and they weren't hurt. I apologized for the bump.

Suddenly one of the women cried out, looking behind me, "My God, your car!"

I looked and saw this incredible sight: my sedan was moving *onto the expressway, directly crossing the Sunday night traffic, turning and making its way to the far barrier.* I expected to hear crashing and squeals of brakes. (As I had slid across the seat to get out on the passenger side, I had knocked the gear from park.) The scene was as if from another dimension. All the oncoming cars stopped; there was no sound. All was silence. Through the rain and looking to the left as I crossed the expressway, I could see a line of car lights as far as the horizon, stopped—and NO ONE WAS BLOWING A HORN. As I came to my car, I saw another one stopped just short of where it would have hit my car. A black man, dressed in black jacket, black slacks, and black shoes, got out and spoke as I reached the car:

"Are you all right?" I said yes and suggested if he could hold the cars back, I could swing mine away from the wall it faced, stopped, with lights on, motor still running. First, I said I must get him some reflective material so no one would strike him while he held them back—but by the time I had pulled some reflective foil from my trunk, he was no longer there. His car and those beside his had pulled back. I was able to swing my car and turn to enter the right-hand lane and go forward. Safely. To this day, I wonder how it could have happened and how I lived through it.

Who were they? Why did no one in that mile-long line of expressway drivers on a dark and rainy night run into anyone else? Blow a horn? When I looked for the women after turning my car around, they had taken off, were nowhere to be seen. Perhaps they thought I was going to be killed, walking across the expressway—as normally I would have been.

The fact that individuals with these qualities would be in this place at this time to me is a lifesaving example of synchronicity.

I recall such a "coincidence" when I needed to get in touch with my younger brother concerning arrangements for my mother in a hospital—but I learned he had left his apartment and could not be reached. He was leaving for South America as part of the Peace Corps, and there was no way to get in touch. As the family was sitting down to dinner, the phone rang. It was my brother, saying he just thought on the spur of the moment he would call to say good-by.

Most of us can recall similar happenings.

Karma can be considered the warp and weft of the loom of existence, guide-threads for the shuttle.

As we see from Al's experiences, what happened in one

life did affect what he met in the others—but it is what he *did* with the circumstances he was given that made the difference.

Dr. Gina Cerminara, who studied the karmic trends in the Edgar Cayce readings, found the effects of past lives on the present very much like those discovered by past-life therapists and regressionists today.

Most of those violent effects were far more frightful than anything Al had experienced—except perhaps for untold parts of the soldier's tale or for possible torture experienced during crucifixion or the briefly mentioned sharkbite when he was swimming in the Mediterranean.

Still, pain can exist without violence. There was no violence mentioned, at least, when young James was forced by his father's men to leave his lover and his son, but the sobs in the remembering voice were real.

Karma is essentially a combination of effects—the effect on human lives of actions with spiritual values—with a purpose of *teaching* by offering appropriate returns for human actions and attitudes. Studying the effects, single and cumulative, of the past lives Al and others experienced makes it evident that there is a system where rewards do come—not so much physical (although Al's delight on the sands of Tripoli was also physical) or monetary (Al never had wealth, though sometimes he lived comfortably), but mental, psychological, spiritual.

Karma can be considered the balancing force which adjusts the weights on the pans of the cosmic pharmacy scale. When we leave one side, the other will be adjusted for the weight we left on the first. Yet we, on either side of the pan, can decide what qualities we will use in dealing with this weight, to make it lighter or heavier, brighter or darker.

Al's lives show, in their development, what Jung describes as "the play of opposites." Jung believed that "psychic energy involves the play of opposites in much the same way as physical energy involves a difference of potential . . . "[9] So there would be a flow of such energy from the "cold" life in Siberia to the "hot" life on the Mediterranean, from the stern and celibate life as the friar to the gentle and well-to-do lover, "James Fitzroy"; even from the brief life as Pierre to the ten times longer life as Jack. Opposites help the energies flow for ultimate balancing.

There is also a constant process of reversal from one kind of personality type to its opposite, Roger Woolger says, as well as "a reversal of moral perspective and major themes . . . So we meet cycles of lives that swing in personality type from concubine to celibate, spendthrift to miser . . . "[10]

Regressionists often encounter changes of sex; Al, however, didn't. When Dr. George asked him to find a life when he was a woman, he replied, "Never was." This would indicate he was comfortable as himself so never chose to experience it, or he never really mistreated the opposite sex enough to have to come back as a woman.

Family relationships occur fairly often, according to professionals. Al, of course, had the same woman as a wife twice—as Brunhilde from the Northland, when he was a Roman soldier, and as Gladys, when he was the investment broker. Each time, she connected him with Christ: converting him to Christianity, as the Roman, and bringing him closer to God, as he said, in the current experience.

William James said that if a combination of experience (or searching for knowledge from it—empiricism) and religion were established, it would bring in a new era, a great awakening. "Let empiricism once become associated with religion, as hitherto, through some strange misunderstanding it has been associated with irreligion, and I believe that a new era of religion as well as of philosophy will be ready to begin."[11]

It is important to recognize not just the interplay and swing of karmic factors in one life after another, but even more important to recognize that *we can do something about it,* by changing something in ourselves that is within our power to change—perhaps as simple as an attitude.

But the great discovery is the discovery of the spirit that moves karma, the spirit behind karma, no mere mechanical adjuster but a spirit which can—as Dr. Tiller suggested—act on and within the physical and the mental. In short, a spirit which embodies the basic meaning of the Greek roots of *psychology:*

PSYCHE: soul or spirit of humanity; base of the will, desires, and passions; heart, soul, mind, understanding.

LOGOS: "the word by which the inward thought is expressed," or "the inward thought" or "reason itself," or the expression of the inner thought of the soul.

This is the spirit that Al felt when he realized there was love behind the lessons he was getting. He, all through his soul's journey, had been touched by that love, had been taught by that spirit, had been held together by that inner thought of the soul. And so had those whom he loved.

It was as if he had felt alone on an island but found he was truly connected, under the water, with a ground of universal caring that included everyone.

> *"No man is an island, entire of itself; every man is a piece of the continent, a part of the main . . . any man's death diminishes me, because I am involved in all mankind."*
>
> —John Donne, *Devotions* XVII

AL TURNER

"Smilin' Al" at work in the office called "the chicken coop" in the A.R.E. headquarters building in 1966.

Appendix

It is possible to find out about past lives—but it is not a task to be taken up on the spur of the moment. Certainly, for the best results, searching should be done prayerfully.

First, it is a good idea to ask yourself why you want to know. Is it mere curiosity? Do you want assurance that you were once Marie Antoinette or Henry VIII or even Marco Polo? Of the hundreds of thousands of past-life recalls, a minuscule number have been well-known characters in history. If that is the reason you want to find out, don't bet on it. You will probably be disappointed.

Of course, it is possible to imagine you were such a person, even daydream about it, but it could be wiser to ask yourself how such daydreaming helps, what does it supply that seems to be missing. As we explore past selves, we may find many different backgrounds, different times, and different countries, but there will be a relationship to this life.

In thousands of individual cases researched by such professionals as Helen Wambach, Bruce Goldberg, Roger Woolger, and Brian Weiss, each one has shown a tie to the present self in some way. Whoever turns up in your background, his or her fear, his or her joy, his or her suffering, his or her talents—and the way that individual looked at life—may give you a new perspective on the present—and opportunities for enriched understanding, seeing more clearly where your real happiness lies.

The chief reason many people are turned toward past lives today is the search for solutions to present problems, whether physical or psychological, solutions that often are not found by searching the present life. For such people the deep source does come to light in lives remembered from past centuries. Once the sources are found and the roots of the problem exposed, healing begins. Perhaps fear of snakes or of the dark or the pain of an aching neck are identified as coming from falling into a snake pit, or being locked in a dungeon, or hanged on a gallows. But when it is recognized that the cause was far back, the cause no longer exists in the present and the problem usually fades away.

People searching for roots of fears should try the present life first, for psychologists say that the great majority of such problems are connected to some event in this life. But, as Dr. Woolger points out, there are often corresponding crises or traumas—such as a childhood injury or adult violent death—in several lives. If there are some problems whose source you can't identify or which ought to vanish with present treatment but don't, that is reason enough for searching the past. It is a healthy motive when you want to search the past to improve the present, to make the present life a better one. Perhaps you may also find other abilities and skills you had in the past and develop them now or learn that certain activities caused trouble for you then—

and it would be wise to avoid them now. There is no telling what may turn up when you look into a past life. Doing it to help yourself in the present, to seek clarity for a spiritual journey, is the most likely motive to bring true satisfaction after the experience.

Entering the experience, you may try it by yourself or with a therapist. By yourself, according to Dr. Weiss, if you head in a potentially troublesome direction with an adverse reaction, your own subconscious may protect you and stop the experience. If anxiety or guilt lingers, a visit to an accredited therapist may relieve the symptoms. An untrained therapist, however, might urge the client right past the warning signals before the person is ready.

If you decide to see a therapist, Dr. Weiss warns, "*I do not recommend past-life therapy done by a therapist who is not certified or accredited by a traditional accrediting body, who does not have a degree such as M.D., Ph.D., M.S.W., or other traditional degree.* Nontraditional past-life therapists may be less likely to let a memory evolve at its own pace and less likely to have the skills necessary to help the patient integrate the material."[1]

A frequent bonus in finding past lives beyond the healing of problems is that experiencing these other backgrounds, whether serf or king, gangster or priest, musician, laborer, or artist, brings a feeling of enhancement, often renewed self-esteem. Elysia, a suburban housewife with grown children, saw herself as a man in the 1890s jailed for an accidental killing; she tried and found great satisfaction in volunteering to tutor at an area prison. Charles, a restless father, found a past life as a Native American; he began working with the Boy Scouts and found unexpected skill in their activities, as well as pleasure and enrichment.

Looking for past-life personalities is a little like going into a mountain wilderness in search of treasure. When you start out on a journey, you are more sure of your travels if you know exactly where you are starting from. Taking a careful look at your present life, what you are doing and what abilities and relationships you have today, then looking backward at your youth, your teens—and don't be too astonished at how far you have changed—and finally looking at your grade school and preschool childhood will take you a little while. But it is worth the time spent. Keep these notes for yourself; you do not have to share them with anyone. You may find out there are far more good points to your personality than you were thinking of during a blue mood.

If you have trouble looking at yourself in this way, try to imagine you are your own best friend, who does not judge you, who is fond of you, but who sees your troubles and triumphs without being personally involved. From the view of this "friend" write down your self-description: your personal strong points, weak points, a recent success, a recent mistake. Write down what is happening now that you feel glad about. Next, what annoys you. This is your "friend's" description of you now.

Then looking at your childhood, what great event—or sad event—might your friend see? Sometimes little flashes of our childhood memories can carry a lot of meaning. Was there something that greatly frustrated you then? Something that scared you or comforted you? Surely there were tribulations in your early school days and maybe a triumph or two. List a couple. Then see what you can recall from the preschool years. What pictures come into your mind? Did you have imaginary playmates? What made you happy? What frightened you?

Some people are reticent and have difficulty expressing themselves freely. If you are one of them, remember that no one needs to see this information but you. It is as private as you want it to be. But it will be helpful later on.

DIFFERENT PATHS TO THE PAST

There are several paths to choose from or you can try them all. The mind has an amazing reach, and parts of the brain are being found to have functions even Freud was not aware of. (The right temporal lobe of the brain, for example, when stimulated, may give an impression of a near-death experience.)[2]

One path is by answering a series of questions designed to ferret out clues about a past personality: physical, psychological, geographical, historical. Most of the questionnaire beginning on page 216 is adapted from the chapter, "How Can I Know My Past Lives?" in *Be Your Own Psychic.*[3] Another path is by using your own sleep state, even the drowsy period, keeping a record of dreams and studying them. A dream journal has many uses, and searching pieces from the past for the jigsaw puzzle of life is one of those uses. Of course, not everything that comes from a dream is necessarily from the past—or from the future, though there are many cases of both. Dreams can also be symbolic, or wishful, or simply clarifying feelings.

A third is with a psychologist or psychiatrist, using past-life regressions as therapy, accessing past experiences by hypnosis. As a rule, therapists first look for sources for an individual's problems in the present life, sometimes even in birth trauma. But if not found there, they can look further back. Sometimes, as in Al's case, problems—even problems in relationships—may go back through centuries. Sometimes the observer part of the subject's personality can select *one* life with a key to the present problem which clears it up. It is important, in choosing a regression therapist, to have one you feel comfortable with, one recommended by someone you trust.

A fourth path is the use of an audiotape especially prepared for regression, usually by a therapist. Dr. Bruce

Goldberg, who did group past-life regression, offered a tape which had age regression on one side, past-life regression on the other. Dr. Brian Weiss offers a script to prepare such a tape in his book, *Through Time into Healing.* Follow the broad suggestions on breathing and relaxation, then for finding a time and a life that will be helpful for you. Picture the details of yourself, the type of clothing, the surroundings—and after the experience, the gentle awakening, feeling refreshed. Dr. Goldberg, when he regressed a group, gave the instruction that if the subjects began to experience something traumatic, they would find themselves outside their bodies, observing what was happening but not feeling it. (A couple of the participants in Dr. Goldberg's session that the author attended did observe their own deaths, but "didn't feel a thing" because of the advance direction.)

Before trying *any* search into the past, it is best to put yourself in a meditative attitude, offer a prayer for love and understanding.

All of the methods below have produced results—with different people. They all involve looking into the storehouse of the mind, storehouses we may unconsciously tap into with our present actions and feelings reacting to some forgotten past.

SEARCHING THROUGH THE ALPHA RHYTHM AND SLEEP STATE

Sometimes it is possible to get a glimpse of a past life even *before* going into a night's sleep. The first stage of somnolence is the alpha state, described by sleep researcher Dr. Julius Segal as "a serene and pleasant relaxation, devoid of concentrated thought."[4] If, before relaxing, we think, "I want to see a scene from a past life," sometimes a picture or sensation will follow on the alpha rhythm.

You may tell yourself, as you prepare for bed, that you

will see a significant scene from your past. You do have "hidden observers," as James Fadiman calls them, parts of your personality which are aware of what you are doing and what you need much of the time. Have your dream recording materials at the bedside in easy reach, then lie down, relaxed, with eyes closed, and let it happen, comfortable in the knowledge that part of you will help while your conscious is asleep. As soon as you are awake, even if it is not yet day, have your pen or pencil and a dim light to write by (a bright one may be too startling), then record anything and everything from the latest dream. (Perception of a dream often changes in retelling or in time, so the sooner it is written, the more accurate it is likely to be.)

DREAM DIALOGUE: A short while after waking, when you have some quiet space, try an exercise where you talk back and forth with the individuals or even with certain objects in your dream. Write down the conversation; it may surprise you. When the conscious fences come down from the subconscious memory, it can offer free thinking that you would not find otherwise, clues to the influence your past has on the present.

For dream searches to be really meaningful, they should be continued over time. If you are not used to writing down dreams, it will usually take a few weeks to become successful at it. But success is worth the effort.

SEARCHING THE PAST FROM QUESTIONS

The following questions were developed to help individuals use their own perception to discover where they might have been, their hidden talents, interests, and psychological blocks. It is best answered after some weeks of prayerful meditation and dream recording. These questions are adapted from those in chapter 3 of *Be Your Own Psychic*, originally developed for an experiment to help individuals discover where they had been, their hidden talents, interests, and psychological blocks.

Physical Qualities:

1. Are there physical types of people to whom you are drawn? by whom you are repelled? Explain.
2. What physical characteristics do you look for and admire in others (either or both sexes)?
3. What is your outstanding body skill?
4. Have you ever disliked a person? What physical characteristics about this person do you remember?
5. Can you recall a physical fight in your experience? Did you win? Did you enjoy it?
6. List the physical habits you make a conscious effort to maintain.
7. What physical habits do you have which are unlike those of most people you know?
8. Describe any personal physical weakness which has persisted or recurred in your experience.
9. How do you feel about this weakness?
10. Is there one of your five senses which is keener than the others? Name it. Give an example.
11. Do you enjoy special sense reactions? Describe them.
12. Are there types of films or videos dealing with a particular type of physical activity which appeal to you? Name one or more.
13. Is there a type of physical activity you find especially exciting, emotionally enjoyable?
14. What particular weakness or physical lack do you complain about most?
15. Is there a particular physical injury or weakness you are afraid of having to face?
16. What physical weakness or handicap do you notice most in others?

17. How do you feel about people mentioned in question #16?

18. What physical ability do you wish for or have you striven to acquire?

Types of Peoples, Foods, Places

19. Do you especially enjoy food(s) of any particular country? Which one(s)?

20. When celebrating, do you seek food of a particular country? Describe, associating food with moods (if possible).

21. Is there any particular way of cooking food you especially enjoy?

22. Do you enjoy cooking food in the open? Do you like food cooked in the open?

23. Have you at any time:
    - Liked long fingernails?
    - Used a good deal of jewelry?
    - Worn your hair in some special fashion? Describe.
    - Attributed great sentimental or real value to some physical object?

24. Is there any race or color of people that attracts you? Explain.

25. Is there any race or color of people that repels you? Explain.

26. Does this interest (#24) express itself in your home decorations, your interest in travel, books you read, etc.? Describe.

27. When you go to a museum, what section do you visit first, and where do you spend the most time?

28. Do you have a special interest in or dislike of any country? Explain.

29. Have you ever visited a particular country and felt immediately at home? Describe.

30. Do you feel drawn to or repelled by any type or group

of people? What do you like or dislike about them?

31. Is there a section of the country which has a strong appeal for you? Explain.

32. Is there a particular type of clothing you feel most comfortable in?

33. Is there a particular type of clothing you strongly dislike wearing?

34. Have you read a historical novel about a country or group of people which strongly appealed to you? Describe briefly.

35. Have you ever had a mystic or transcendent experience? Describe its nature and your age when it happened.

36. What is your most absorbing hobby or special interest at present?

37. How much time do you spend on it weekly?

38. How many people do you know who have the same hobby or interest?

39. Do you have intense feelings of excitement or enjoyment from any type of group games or activities? Explain.

40. How much time do you spend alone daily? Do you enjoy being alone?

41. Do you make an effort to be alone in the out-of-doors? Do you spend much time reading or in libraries?

42. Is there a problem which occurs frequently in your experience? Describe.

43. Is there some favorable event or condition which recurs? Describe briefly.

44. What faults do you notice most in others?

45. What weaknesses do you notice most in others?

46. Is there any type of person you are afraid of?

47. Is there any experience or activity you are afraid of? Describe.

48. What do you fear most?

49. What annoys you most?

50. What type of music do you like most?

51. How frequently do you listen to it (daily, weekly)?

52. Do you recall an outstanding emotional experience related to music? Describe the music and the experience, and your age when it happened, and where.

53. Has any of your dreams been repeated three or more times? Describe.

54. Have you ever felt a sudden attraction to a person? Describe the person.

55. Have you ever visited for the first time a place you then found familiar?

56. Do you speak one or more foreign languages? Which? Which is your favorite?

57. Do you like songs of any particular country? Which?

58. Are there songs that make you feel sad? Explain.

59. Is there a particular type of person you try to avoid?

60. Is there a particular type of person you like to be with? Explain.

Set the answers to those questions aside for a few days, then bring them out and look for the connections. "Diane" found she had a keen sense of hearing, enjoyed music, particularly religious, even Gregorian hymns. She enjoyed tea with milk, and roast beef dinners. She wore her long hair in a plain bun much of the time, and chose dresses in plain materials. And she recalled being sent to a speech therapist in second grade because they had trouble understanding her "British accent." Might she have been a nun in England in the days of Jane Eyre (one of her favorite books)?

"Marie" always went to the Chinese section of a museum to see their carvings, their art. She enjoyed Chinese food. She never was much for walking; her feet were often hurting. She was frightened by people who were very fat. Could she have had a Chinese life with an unhappy ending?

"George" tried a tape for a past life. Asked what he was wearing, he visualized tights and a tunic, something like the pages in an old castle. He was a favorite of a nobleman. When he progressed forward a few more years, he found himself in a prison, straw on the floor, a tiny window for light. A man was coming toward him with a hot poker. Then he was outside his body, watching the prisoner impersonally. "George" was born with one eye slightly tilted. Was this a remnant of torture in an old life?

IS KARMA WORKING IN PEOPLE AND THE WORLD?

"Judith" was seeing a therapist for her anorexia, which had come on recently and had brought her weight down to eighty pounds when she had been 120. She recalled being a stout and powerful politician, who liked slim women, but also mistreated them. Whether or not she understood the significance of taking the place of the one she had previously injured, this knowledge enabled her to see the fault in her past and, realizing it was no longer part of her present, she came back to health in a few weeks.

"Tom," a young man just out of high school with emotional problems, learned that in one past life in Shakespearean England he had played the part of women on the stage. Wearing the outfit off the stage, he had been captured and tormented by a bully. Looking at that experience, he tried to dress exactly as he wanted to be perceived—not just as his friends dressed—and fit in more comfortably at his job.

As we could see from Al's series of lives, it was not just deeds that lined up karmic repayment, but attitudes. If a person despised a type of man because of prejudice, as Al did the Roman soldiers, he could return as just the type he despised, so he would know what *that* experience was like. (In *Finian's Rainbow,* we recall that a leprechaun turns the overbearing white Southern politician into a black man who learns his lesson and—in the present, not a future life—comes back to his former status.)

Therapists and researchers today bear out what the Edgar Cayce readings state: Past lives, past incarnations in the earth plane, play an important part in the total emotional life of an individual.

Some psychologists today speak of the "karmic swing" for case histories where the person is bullied and beaten in one life, in the next *he* or *she* does the abusing, and next may again be the one to be hurt. A succession of past lives will show it again and again—with a change when the individual realizes there is a greater good, a better way. According to the Cayce readings, karma is a very definite law. An individual at any point is the sum total of all experiences in every plane of consciousness. This is, in fact, an ancient belief as well. From Hippocrates, from ancient Buddhist teachings, even the Maya, the past is an integral part of the present.

We seem to be reaching further today, granting that the subconscious mind records minute detail far beyond physical consciousness. Scientists such as Dr. William Tiller are now advancing the proposition that consciousness does exist at the *cell level, even in the energy level.*

Emotions are, of course, a form of psychological energy. By finding reasons behind the emotions in the past, it has been possible to change or remove some negative or fearful ones. One example was the client of psychiatrist Denys Kelsey, mentioned in chapter 15, who suffered severely from a phobia of feathers. He could not stand to see or be near any, not even a pillow. The source was found to be a past life in the Foreign Legion where he had been in a battle, then was left for dead in the desert—but while he was still barely alive, vultures had found him. Knowing the horror that caused the phobia enabled the client to move past it, to leave the past in the past, and enjoy the present.

Sometimes it is not just a psychological problem or fear that is removed, it can be a physical problem as well—if that problem was caused by the mind acting on the body; and we now know that that is constantly happening. It was surprising to Claire when her five-year-old son said, while his eyes were closed and he was thinking of a time he had been a soldier, to hear him say he was wounded in the wrist. After he was assured that that was all in the past, a problem he had with eczema persisting in that wrist gradually disappeared.

Déjà vu—meaning "already seen"—is an experience of recognizing something as being familiar though it was not seen before. This has been reported many times and may be a clue to a previous life. General Patton, in his biography, told of a time in France when he "recognized" a spot which had been a Roman encampment centuries earlier. Grace, on a trip to Sedona, Arizona, "recognized" a red rock area on the Airport Mesa as the scene of ancient lovemaking. Grace's husband, in his sleep, sometimes chanted Indian words. Had they known each other in a former life?

Paul and Susan, touring England with their three-year-old Billy, were visiting Warwick Castle. As they descended some steps to a hallway which led to a dungeon, Billy began to panic. There was nothing about the plain hallway to remind anyone of a dungeon. Yet the child screamed and struggled violently. One parent had to take him outside and wait; they had to take turns, one visiting the dungeon, while the other stayed outside with the three year old, who had been just fine in every other part of the castle they visited. Had he once been in the inner cell—or worse, in the cell beneath that one, accessible only through a trapdoor with a metal grate, where a prisoner was doomed to stay, unnoticed and unheard, fed only by what might be dropped through the trapdoor? No one discussed it in Billy's presence, but he seemed to know.

All of these ways of looking into the past, through the subconscious or whatever you wish to call the part of the soul-mind that goes beyond limiting space and time, are tools. They are not goals in themselves.

Seeking with spiritual guidance as we use these tools will help, as it did with Al, to make progress on the journey. We, too, are on a path toward "the Light," going forward or backward or standing still. It is our own free will—as said in Deuteronomy 30:15-19—that makes the choices, in the past for the present, and in the present for the future.

ARE THESE EXAMPLES OF REINCARNATION THROUGH HISTORY?

If indeed karma, as a balancing of life, and dharma, as a principle of grace, have been operating through history, we would expect to find numerous times when people who act with disregard of others might be born later to be themselves disregarded.

A primitive, but easily visible example is warring tribes: the tribe which defeats another cruelly is, after time, defeated—if not by its victims, by others—with equal cruelty.

The Greeks, who developed high technology for the fifth and fourth centuries B.C., but fought fairly civilized battles for that age, were later defeated—in a fairly civilized manner—as the Romans took over that area with many others. But Greeks were hired to teach young Roman nobles, and many Roman youths went to Greece for their "higher education."

So long as the Romans treated conquered peoples with comparative consideration, they flourished, but as bribery and corruption increased from Tiberius on, their treatment of foreign peoples deteriorated, and Goths, Visigoths, and Vandals brought a savage takeover.

In other parts of the world, in Asia, Africa, the Americas,

this same rise and fall was taking place. The Mayan people, who originated probably from the ancient Olmec in Mexico and Central America from around 1,000 B.C. developed a civilization of wide trade and power by 800 A.D., but used what we consider today barbaric practices. By 1,000 A.D. there were few signs that a great people had once been there. The few groups that were unified were conquered in the 1500s by Spanish explorers, with their thirst for compulsive conversion of people to their "Christian" religion. The bishop, Diego de Landa, gathered hundreds of preserved Mayan records written as "bark" books, carefully illustrated—and burned all but four, which found their way to Europe.

It is interesting to wonder whether people who were tortured by the Inquisition had themselves been torturers in the past. There was ample opportunity in Europe in the fifteenth and sixteenth centuries for all kinds of cruelty.

Coming closer to the present, there are constant reminders around the globe that oppressors eventually get oppressed themselves, such as the tumbling of the Russian czars and the rise of the Communists, then the apparent tumbling of the Communists and the rise of—what?

There was a love for power under the Kaiser, then the defeat of Germany after the First World War, and the economic revenge taken on that country by its conquerors—which led to a national mood that welcomed a young Nazi, who rallied them to take their place in the sun as the "master race." (It is interesting that the root word for the titles *czar* and *kaiser* is the same: CAESAR. And we can search through world governments without finding that title today.)

It seems possible that not only individuals but nations as well affect their futures by what they do in the present.

Notes

Introduction

1. Matthew 16:14, Mark 6:15, Luke 9:8-9, John 9:2.

2. Woolger, Roger J., *Other Lives, Other Selves,* Doubleday, 1987, p. 31.

3. This Congress was held in Montreal, June 22-25, 1993.

Chapter 1

1. *Through Time into Healing,* Brian L. Weiss, p. 54.

Chapter 2

1. From a conversation with Carol Bowman, after reading her article, "Exploring Past-Life Memories with Children," *Venture Inward,* July/August, 1993.

2. Marcuse, F. L., Ph.D., *Hypnosis,* Penguin Books, 1959.

3. Should he have spoken in French? It seems that most hypnotized subjects, certainly those of the regressionists cited earlier, would normally use the language their brain is most familiar with, even though they are in a "lifetime" in a foreign country, unless they are specifically asked to speak in the foreign tongue.

Chapter 3

1. These glimpses into Al's thoughts are based in part on conversations with Gladys, in part on observing his way of life, and sharing weeks with him and Gladys in Virginia Beach in the late fifties and sixties.

2. The addresses, including streets, were checked not for absolute accuracy—even the best of us may not remember ten or fifteen years later some address we visited—but for probability. If there were no addresses beginning with "Spice—" we would have no indication it might be real. However, because the 1993 map of Richmond streets included Spicewood several times—e.g. Circle, Drive, Court, and Point, there might well have been a Spice . . . Street then.

3. See chapter 11, where the Tripolitan had no use for women because a powerful woman (Egyptian princess) had whipped his father to death, leaving the son with a total distaste for women.

4. This is highly probable. The 1993 Toronto street map showed some twenty-four streets beginning with Bell—from Bell Manor Drive and Belle Ayre Blvd. to Bellwoods Place.

Chapter 4

1. The worst period of the panic was the following year, 1873, according to the Financial Record and *The Curbstone Brokers*, "The Origins of the American Stock Exchange," pp. 63 and 93, by Robert Sobel, Macmillan, 1970.

2. Historical researcher Robert Swartz found six types of Civil War rifles which began with a G: Gwyn and Campbell (a carbine), Gallagher, George Army, Greenwood and Gray, and Greene; but no "Grand Rapids." Al spoke of the rifle again in the fourth session: "A rifle named 'Grand Union,' No. 36,521." This recollection appears to be the type of memory "confabulation" mentioned by Dr. Roger Woolger, where the event is true but some details are fantasy.

3. Samuel (Sam) Houston, 1793-1863, was a general; president of the Republic of Texas, 1836-1838 and 1841-1844; U.S. senator, 1846-1859.

4. The records for this period in the Philadelphia City Archives at 401 N. Broad St. were practically illegible.

Chapter 5

1. It could be remarkable enough for a man with no education beyond high school to come up with the right king for this time period, let alone the other similarities. This king was James I of England, but he was James VI of Scotland from the year 1567 when he was one year old; in 1603 he became James I of England as well.

2. *King James: VI of Scotland, I of England,* by Antonia Fraser; pp. 40-44, Alfred Knopf, 1975; *This Realm of England, 1399-1688,* p. 284, Lacey Baldwin Smith, D. C. Heath, 1966.

3. Edgar Cayce reading 288-27.

4. *Many Happy Returns,* by W. H. Church, Harper & Row, 1984.

5. *The Bible, in Its Ancient and English Versions,* edited by H. Wheeler Robinson, Clarendon Press, Oxford, 1940, p. 202.

6. There were six committees of learned men called by their bishops for the translation: two meeting at Oxford, two at Cambridge, and two at Westminster. "The king had appointed certain men, to the number of four and fifty, for the translation of the Bible." *The Bible in Its Ancient and English Versions, op. cit.,* p. 198.

Chapter 6

1. Reading 3460-1.

Chapter 7

1. Later on, he says of the fish, "We would net them."

2. A correspondent in the Philippines some years ago sent me a gift of several yards of cloth made from the bark of a tree.

Chapter 8

1. This would be within the range of the Sikhote-Alin Mountains, near Tatarsk Strait, connecting with the Sea of Okhotsk. Probably it was far enough inland so there was no moderating effect on the temperature by the large sea. Fifty degrees below zero is a common temperature in Siberian winters, according to *Siberia,* by George St. George, D. McKay, 1969.

2. *Encyclopedia of Mammals,* Dr. David MacDonald, ed. Facts-on-File Publications, copyright 1984, reprinted 1985.

3. The *Encyclopaedia Britannica*, "Siberian Artistic Expression," vol. 16, 15th edition, p. 726.

4. *Encyclopedia of Religion*, vol. 15, pp. 493-495.

5. *Ibid.*, pp. 494-495.

6. The Bible. *Old Testament*, I Kings 19:12.

Chapter 9

1. Pontius Pilate was the Roman governor of Judaea.

2. Dr. Samuel T. Lachs, rabbi and now retired professor of religion at Bryn Mawr College, spoke of this in a lecture at Bryn Mawr College in 1984. He gives in-depth information in his book, *A Rabbinic Commentary on the New Testament—Matthew, Mark, and Luke*, published by KTAV, Hoboken, N.J., in 1987.

3. James Fadiman, Ph.D., *Awareness of Personal Multiplicities*, lecture, Montreal, Quebec, 22 June 1993. Dr. Fadiman is a California psychologist.

4. Acts 15:22.

5. John 4:6-30, the story of the woman of Samaria who met Jesus at Jacob's well. After an exchange of conversation about the well water and the water of life, she asked Him to give her *that* special water. Jesus told her to call her husband; she said, "I have no husband," and Jesus replied, "Thou hast well said, I have no husband: For thou hast had five husbands; and he whom thou now hast is not thy husband . . . "

6. Judd, Gerrit P., ed., *A History of Civilization*, Macmillan, 1966, p. 27.

7. *Encyclopaedia Britannica*, *Micropedia*, vol. 1, p. 476.

8. Some individuals' eyes are far more sensitive than others. They can detect the radiation of some kinds of energy, including the magnetic energy of the body, which is described as the human aura. This has been called the basis of the halos and sometimes the glow painted by artists around saints. Shafica Karagulla, M.D., gives a detailed re-

port of these phenomena in her book, *Breakthrough to Creativity*, the chapter on "Three Energy Fields Around Human Beings," DeVores, Inc., 1967, pp. 158-170.

9. Mark 3:7-10.

10. Matthew 5:22. "But I say unto you, That whosoever is angry with his brother without a cause shall be in danger of the judgment: and whosoever shall say to his brother, Raca [vain fellow], shall be in danger of the council: but whosoever shall say, Thou fool, shall be in danger of hell fire." (King James Version)

11. During the papacy of Pope Pius XII (1939-1958), shortly after World War II, what was believed to be the tomb of St. Peter was discovered in excavations near the Vatican. We have not heard of a tomb of Achmesh or Stephen.

Chapter 10

1. *New College Latin and English Dictionary*, John Traupman, Bantam.

2. Judd, *op. cit.*, p. 84.

3. Judd, *op. cit.*, p. 94.

4. Judd, *op. cit.*, p. 96.

5. Judd, *op. cit.*, p. 85.

6. Ra, or Ra Ta, was a high priest in one of the first couple of Egyptian dynasties and, according to the readings, one of Cayce's own earliest appearances on earth.

7. W. H. Church, *Many Happy Returns*, p. 60, notes 2 and 3, cited reading 294-147 for Edgar Cayce's Egyptian birth as Ra Ta, the name "means and indicates among—or the first *pure* white in the experience then of the earth." Church suggests that this date approximates 10,600 B.C.

8. When Al was a youth in high school, his closest and favorite brother was named Paul; Paul was killed in an accident when Al was only fifteen.

9. The author majored in Latin at Bryn Mawr College and had three years of graduate courses in it.

Chapter 11

1. *What Wood Is That?* Herbert L. Edlin, Viking Press, 1969, pp. 106-109.

2. Onan: The name means "strong." See Genesis 38:4.

3. A shekel was an ancient weight unit used by the Hebrews, Babylonians, etc., equal to about half an ounce; also, a half-ounce gold or silver coin of the ancient Hebrews.

4. There are several reported instances of light around someone who has just died. In *A Man Called Peter,* Catherine Marshall describes the light around her husband right afterward. At a 1992 meeting of Delaware Valley Near-Death Studies, three people, including Mrs. Cunningham of Wayne, Pa., reported light around a family member who had just passed on.

5. In speaking about the first soul created, Edgar Cayce's psychic readings indicated that that was one who entered the earth for the purpose of helping those who had become trapped in matter. "The name of that soul then was Amilius, and its sojourn in the earth was in spirit form only." *Lives of the Master,* Glenn Sanderfur, p. 40. Also, quoting from Cayce reading 364-7, "(Q) Please give the important reincarnations of Adam in the world's history. (A) In the beginning as Amilius . . . "

Chapter 12

1. A number of them have spoken for Temple University's Center for Frontier Sciences, Philadelphia, Pa. Beverly Rubik, Ph.D., director, also publishes a journal for the Center.

Chapter 13

1. This chapter includes some material from *The Light in the Mirror* (Dorrance, 1985), a family biography.

2. *Other Lives, Other Selves,* Roger J. Woolger, Ph.D., Bantam, N.Y., 1988, pp. 96 ff.

3. *Webster's New World Dictionary of the American Language*, World Publishing Co., N.Y., 1957.

4. *There Is a River*, Thomas Sugrue, Holt, Rinehart and Winston, New York, N.Y., 1973, pp. 320-321.

Chapter 14

1. Much of the material in this chapter is adapted from the author's family biography of Al, *The Light in the Mirror*, 1985.

2. Copyright 1968, Association for Research and Enlightenment, Inc.

Chapter 15

1. Exodus 21:24.

2. See bibliography, specifically works of Bryan Weiss, M.D.; Roger Woolger, Ph.D.; Helen Wambach, Ph.D.; Bruce Goldberg, D.D.S.; Gina Cerminara, Ph.D.; Ian Stevenson, M.D.

3. Dr. Leslie Weatherhead has a worthy comment on this verse from John 9:3: Jesus' answer does not mean that the man had to be blind so long just to give Jesus a chance to show His power; the full stop in the sentence should come after the word "parents" but the translator had no punctuation in the manuscript. So the words should be read, "Neither hath this man sinned nor his parents." (full stop) "But, that the works of God should be made manifest in him, I must work the works of him that sent me while it is day." This seems to say that sin is not involved here, that the job is just to get the man cured before night. *The Christian Agnostic*, p. 295.

4. Woolger, Roger J. *Other Lives, Other Selves*, p. 212.

5. For information on this program, contact U.S. Association for Victim-Offender Mediation, Administrative Offices, PACT Institute of Justice, 254 S. Morgan Boulevard, Valparaiso, Indiana 46383; phone (219)462-1127.

6. The magazine of the Association for Research and Enlightenment, Inc., and the Edgar Cayce Foundation.

7. Woolger, *op. cit.*

8. William A. Tiller, Ph.D., in a lecture to the Center of Frontier Sciences, Temple University, September 28, 1993, "Subtle Energies: What Are They, and How Are They Important in the Emerging Field of Energy Medicine." Dr. Tiller has worked in the field of materials science research, which he did in Westinghouse Research Laboratory for nine years, and is professor of engineering sciences at Stanford University, has published 250 papers in that area plus three technical books, and has also spent thirty years in the frontier science area of psychoenergetic research, on which he has published sixty papers.

Ancient Greek mythology referred constantly to spirits inhabiting plants, trees, earth, sky, and sea. The Greek physician, Hippocrates, called "the Father of Medicine," worked with a form of "subtle energies."

9. Jung, Carl Gustaf, *Modern Man in Search of a Soul*, Routledge & Kegan Paul, London, 1953.

10. Woolger, *op. cit.*, p. 218.

11. James, William, *A Pluralistic Universe.* Longmans, Green, N.Y., 1912, p. 314.

Appendix

1. Dr. Brian Weiss, *Through Time into Healing*, Simon & Schuster, 1992.

2. Dr. Elizabeth Blackmore, quoted in *The Philadelphia Inquirer*, October 17, 1992.

3. Patterson and Shelley, *Be Your Own Psychic*, A.R.E. Press, Virginia Beach, 1975, pp. 21-26.

4. Gay Gaer Luce and Dr. Julius Segal, *Sleep*, Coward McCann, 1966.

Bibliography

Bernstein, Morey. *The Search for Bridey Murphy,* Doubleday, New York, N.Y., 1956.

Cerminara, Gina. *Many Mansions,* William Sloane Associates, Inc., New York, N.Y., 1950.

Church, W. H. *Many Happy Returns: The Lives of Edgar Cayce,* Harper & Row, San Francisco, Calif., 1984.

Fraser, Antonia. *King James: VI of Scotland, I of England,* Alfred A. Knopf, New York, N.Y., 1975.

Goldberg, Dr. Bruce. *Past Lives, Future Lives,* Ballantine Books, New York, N.Y., 1982.

Grof, Stanislav, M.D.; Cayce, Hugh Lynn; Johnson, Raynor C., Ph.D. *Dimensions of Dying and Rebirth,* A.R.E. Press, Virginia Beach, Va., 1977.

James, William. *A Pluralistic Universe,* Longmans, Green & Co., New York, N.Y., 1912.

Judd, Gerrit P. *A History of Civilization,* Macmillan Co., New York, N.Y., 1966.

Judge, William Q. *The Scope of Reincarnation,* Cunningham Press, Alhambra, Calif., 1960.

Jung, C.G. *Memories, Dreams, Reflections,* recorded and edited by Aniela Jaffe, Vintage Books, Random House, New York, N.Y., 1961.

Jung, C. G. *Modern Man in Search of a Soul,* Routledge & Kegan Paul, Ltd., London, England, 1933.

Kelsey, Denys, M.B., M.R.C.P., and Grant, Joan. *Many Lifetimes,* Doubleday, New York, N.Y., 1967.

Kempe, Frederick. *Siberian Odyssey: A Voyage into the Rus-*

sian Soul, G. P. Putnam & Sons, New York, N.Y., 1992.

Luce, Gay Gaer, and Segal, Julius, M.D. *Sleep.* Coward McCann, Inc., New York, N.Y., 1966.

MacDonald, David, ed. *Encyclopedia of Mammals,* Facts on File Pub., 1984.

Marcuse, F. L. *Hypnosis: Fact and Fiction,* Penguin Books, Baltimore, Md., 1959.

Moody, Raymond A., Jr., M.D., with Perry, Paul. *Coming Back: A Psychiatrist Explores Past-Life Journeys,* Bantam, New York, N.Y., 1991.

Obergethmann, Hans. *This Is Italy,* R. Oldenbourg, Graphische Betriebe Gmbh, Munich, Germany.

Patterson, Doris T., and Shelley, Violet M. *Be Your Own Psychic,* A.R.E. Press, Virginia Beach, Va., 1975.

Sliker, Gretchen. *Multiple Mind: Healing the Split in Psyche and World,* Shambhala Publishers, Boston, Mass., 1992.

Smith, Lacey Baldwin. *This Realm of England: 1399-1688,* D. C. Heath, Lexington, Ky., 1966.

St. George, George. *Siberia,* D. McKay Company, New York, N.Y., 1969.

Stevenson, Ian, M.D. *Twenty Cases Suggestive of Reincarnation,* American Society for Psychical Research, New York, N.Y., 1966.

Sugrue, Thomas. *There Is a River: The Story of Edgar Cayce,* Henry Holt, New York, N.Y., 1942.

Wambach, Helen. *Reliving Past Lives: The Evidence Under Hypnosis,* Harper & Row, New York, N.Y., 1978.

Weatherhead, Leslie D. *The Christian Agnostic,* Abingdon Press, Nashville, Tenn., 1965.

Weiss, Brian L., M.D. *Many Lives, Many Masters,* Simon & Schuster, New York, N.Y., 1988.

Weiss, Brian L., M.D. *Through Time into Healing,* Simon & Schuster, New York, N.Y., 1992.

Wilson, Colin. *The Occult: A History,* Random House, N.Y., 1971.

Woolger, Roger J. *Other Lives, Other Selves: A Jungian Psychotherapist Discovers Past Lives,* Doubleday, New York, N.Y., 1987.

ABOUT THE AUTHOR

Doris Patterson has been researching lives in other periods of history since she went to Bryn Mawr College, where her honors project was the biography of a woman of ancient Rome, with an appendix of love letters—in Latin.

Her first story was published after the birth of her first child, her first book (*Your Family Goes Camping*) after the birth of her fourth. Introduced to the A.R.E. by her Uncle Al, she has written two publications for them: *The Unfettered Mind: Varieties of ESP in the Edgar Cayce Readings* and *Be Your Own Psychic*, with Violet Shelley. She also wrote a biography of Al Turner, *The Light in the Mirror*, for family and friends. She taught Latin for a decade, received her M.Ed. in educational media, and continued research into past lives, lecturing on psychic phenomena and writing for newspapers and magazines. She is a volunteer tutor in a maximum security prison, a member of "Community Watch," and past president of Delaware Valley Near-Death Studies, Inc. When her husband, Bill, died nine months after his near-death experience, she studied further and experienced her own past-life regression. Now a widow and grandmother of eight, she finds her past lives helpful in avoiding some pitfalls in the present.

A.R.E. Press

A.R.E. Press is a publisher and distributor of books, audiotapes, and videos that offer guidance for a more fulfilling life. Our products are based on, or are compatible with, the concepts in the psychic readings of Edgar Cayce.

We especially seek to create products which carry forward the inspirational story of individuals who have made practical application of the Cayce legacy.

For a free catalog, please write to A.R.E. Press at the address below or call toll free 1-800-723-1112. For any other information, please call 804-428-3588.

A.R.E. Press
Sixty-Eighth & Atlantic Avenue
P.O. Box 656
Virginia Beach, VA 23451-0656

What Is A.R.E.?

The Association for Research and Enlightenment, Inc. (A.R.E.®), is the international headquarters for the work of Edgar Cayce (1877-1945), who is considered the best-documented psychic of the twentieth century. Founded in 1931, the A.R.E. consists of a community of people from all walks of life and spiritual traditions, who have found meaningful and life-transformative insights from the readings of Edgar Cayce.

Although A.R.E. headquarters is located in Virginia Beach, Virginia—where visitors are always welcome—the A.R.E. community is a global network of individuals who offer conferences, educational activities, and fellowship around the world. People of every age are invited to participate in programs that focus on such topics as holistic health, dreams, reincarnation, ESP, the power of the mind, meditation, and personal spirituality.

In addition to study groups and various activities, the A.R.E. offers membership benefits and services, a bimonthly magazine, a newsletter, extracts from the Cayce readings, conferences, international tours, a massage school curriculum, an impressive volunteer network, a retreat-type camp for children and adults, and A.R.E. contacts around the world. A.R.E. also maintains an affiliation with Atlantic University, which offers a master's degree program in Transpersonal Studies.

For additional information about A.R.E. activities hosted near you, please contact:

A.R.E.
67th St. and Atlantic Ave.
P.O. Box 595
Virginia Beach, VA 23451-0595
(804) 428-3588